Making Community Connections

Connie L. Knapp and
The Orton Family Foundation Community Mapping Program

ESRI PRESS
REDLANDS, CALIFORNIA

First printing November 2003.

Printed in the United States of America.

Library of Congress Cataloging-in-Publication Data
Making community connections : the Orton Family Foundation community mapping program.
    p. cm.
    ISBN 1-58948-071-6 (pbk. : alk. paper)
    1. Student service--United States. 2. Community and school--United States. 3. Young volunteers in community development--United States. 4. Cartography--Study and teaching--United States. 5. Orton Family Foundation.
  LC220.5.M35 2003
  361.3'7--dc22   2003024288

Published by ESRI, 380 New York Street, Redlands, California 92373-8100.

Books from ESRI Press are available to resellers worldwide through Independent Publishers Group (IPG). For information on volume discounts, or to place an order, call IPG at 1-800-888-4741 in the United States, or at 312-337-0747 outside the United States.

Contents

Acknowledgments

This book was made possible through the tremendous enthusiasm and thoughtful contributions of our partners: the teachers, students, and community partners who pursued Community Mapping projects in their schools and communities these past four years. Their interest in studying local places and dedication to making the projects a meaningful learning experience that had application and value in the real world was truly inspiring. We would like to particularly recognize David Smith, GIS instructor; Dr. Sally Wither, place-based curriculum and assessments specialist; Marcia Martin, project design and management instructor; Dr. Joseph J. Kerski, U.S. Geologic Survey; Libbie Miller, Colorado Division of Wildlife; Dr. Cyndy Simms, Superintendent of Steamboat Springs Schools; Cynthia Faughnan of Hartford (Vermont) Memorial Middle School; and Dan Beaupre, Education Quests.

A special thanks and acknowledgment goes to our very first and most important partner, the Vermont Institute of Natural Science (VINS). Ned Swanberg, Nicole Conte, Andy Toepfer, and Erin Flather of VINS have worked with us from the beginning to build a strong, innovative program—they have given their minds and hearts to this work. We also thank the Yampa Valley Legacy Education Initiative (an Annenberg Rural Challenge project) for funding our Colorado work in 1999 and 2000 and Towny Anderson, formerly of The Orton Family Foundation, for getting the Colorado program off the ground. We are also deeply indebted to Lyman Orton: his vision, regard for youth as citizens in our communities, and emphasis on the importance of place helped drive this program from dream to reality. Bill Shouldice's support of our work and unflagging dedication to meaningful engagement by youth and adults in the futures of their communities was similarly invaluable.

Prepublication reviewers Dace Carver, Sophia Linn, and Barbara Ann Richman improved the book in crucial ways.

Finally we want to thank ESRI for its inspiring k-12 work. George Dailey and Charlie Fitzpatrick are truly in a league of their own and ESRI's publication of this book is most appreciated. We are grateful to ESRI Press: editor Gary Amdahl, designer Jennifer Galloway, cover artist Savitri Brant, and copy editor Tiffany Wilkerson for their tremendous work in making this book come to life, and to Esther Worker for supporting our growing needs on the ground.

William Roper
Director of Programs, The Orton Family Foundation

About the Foundation

Any small community is very much a part of the modern world. Facing ever-changing economic, social, and environmental pressures, its citizens are challenged to envision, plan for, and create a future that will protect and enhance their quality of life for generations to come. Though the challenges are daunting, rural communities have found a trusted resource in The Orton Family Foundation. Since 1995, it has developed planning tools that help rural communities define and build healthy, vibrant, and sustainable futures while preserving their heritage.

As a not-for-profit, private operating foundation supported by profits from the Vermont Country Store, The Orton Family Foundation provides innovative tools that facilitate decision making within local communities. The tools include educational programs, workshops, publications, video presentations, software products, and other planning resources. All of the Foundation's tools are designed to help communities:

- build consensus in the planning process
- enhance the predictability of the development planning and approvals process
- facilitate timely decision making
- benefit from information on the latest, proven techniques in community planning

Because the Foundation believes that local community members are best suited to understand local needs and goals, it advocates no particular point of view, approach, nor agenda; instead The Orton Family Foundation is a facilitator of the citizen participation process and seeks to enable communities to define and achieve the future they desire. For more information visit *www.orton.org.*

Foreword

Dr. Joseph J. Kerski
Geographer, U. S. Geological Survey

Introduction

Making Community Connections is a success story. For several years, The Orton Family Foundation has been helping students, training teachers, and working with geographic information systems (GIS), global positioning systems (GPS), and other spatial technologies to help communities examine local issues and plan for their future. Similar to GIS professionals who have been quietly revolutionizing twenty-first century decision making, The Orton Family Foundation has been transforming citizen involvement and student learning community by community.

For centuries, scientists and educational theorists have advocated a method of learning that is based on direct observation of phenomena. Aristotle (born 384 B.C.) initiated these methods, which were revived and refined 2,000 years later by Rousseau (born 1712 in Geneva) and Pestalozzi (born 1746 in the Swiss Republic). Pestalozzi championed a look-and-see approach that he tested in a series of schools that he opened until his death in 1827. More recently, educational journals, popular magazines, and newspaper editorials alike have advocated learning that is focused on observations and measurements in the real world, using community-based issues. Top-down programs from federal and state departments of education, as well as grassroots programs from parents and citizens have each tried to involve students in local, field-based learning through a variety of programs over this same time period. Some have been successful, and some have not. What makes the Community Mapping Program (CMP) different from other programs that have had similar goals of providing students with project and community-based learning experiences?

Reasons for success

First, CMP is a grassroots program but with an organization behind it, The Orton Family Foundation. In a survey that I conducted of 1,520 secondary school teachers who use GIS, respondents expressed their dismay about the lack of a sustained, coordinated program that could provide them assistance when they need it. CMP provides that support, thus ensuring a sustainable program. The mission of The Orton Family Foundation is to help citizens of small towns and cities define their future, shape their growth, and preserve the heritage of their communities and their surroundings. With sprawl spreading far from metropolitan areas into rural communities that have seen very little change until recently, this program could not have come at a better time.

Second, in today's educational environment, if a program does not adhere to national and state academic standards, it will not be used in the classroom. CMP adheres to standards in geography, history, mathematics, reading and writing, science, civics, and visual arts. The program also is grounded in established learning theory.

In addition, CMP represents an excellent model of the geographic inquiry process advocated in the national geography academic standards, Geography For Life. By working with a Community Mapping (CM) project, the students cannot help but ask geographic questions, because these questions form the basis of each project. They must acquire geographic resources through digital maps, aerial photographs, satellite images, tabular data, coordinates from their GPS units, and other means. They are required to explore and analyze geographic information that speaks to the issues they are studying. Finally, they act on geographic knowledge by presenting their results and recommendations to each other and to the community. CM projects can readily lead to more questions, which in turn may start the inquiry process all over again, just as it does for decision makers all over the world.

Because of the place-based nature of the Community Mapping Program, the need for a technology that allows for the visualization of outcomes, and a requirement to examine both the cultural and physical landscape, GIS was a logical requirement for the program. However, even though CM projects involve technology, *Making Community Connections* makes it clear that the map generated by the student is not the end product—it is the beginning of inquiring about the issue.

Thus, the needs drive the technology, not the other way around. GIS, GPS, visualization tools, remote sensing, and other technologies and tools are critically important, but they are used with the goal of understanding the community, not understanding GIS. In addition, the program stresses that teachers and students do not need to know everything about geographic information science to use GIS software. The CMP approach is not *How do we get GIS into the curriculum?*, but to ask, *How can GIS help my students to understand our community?*

The principles of incorporating GIS, GPS, and remote sensing technologies and methods advocated in this book are very much the ones to which I espouse because I have seen them work, time after time. Training a group of teachers who can go out and train others, focusing on a local issue, moving quickly to hands-on work, and providing teacher incentives are a few of these excellent principles. They provide a roadmap, not a toolbox. This is evident in this book's practical advice. For example, it suggests not explaining every GIS pull-down menu and tool in a training session. These menus and tools do not make sense to participants until they have to use them in the context of a lesson or real-life project.

The final reason why I believe that CMP should be used in the curriculum is that the program, quite simply, works. I have worked side-by-side teaching with the staff of The Orton Family Foundation since the late 1990s. I have attended their workshops. I have talked with students who have been in CM programs. It works.

The authors seem to have left a strand of humility throughout the book that I find refreshing. They recognize that there are many pathways to involving students in community-based issues through geographic techniques and methods. In fact, their long-range goal is for schools to become less dependent on CMP staff to sustain the work that they have begun in these communities. Upon starting the Community Mapping Program, the organizers did not rush out and write a book. Rather, this book is the careful result of four years of their observations, practice, and research. I know that the heart of the staff is in the right place—they have a passion for growing the knowledge, skills, and involvement of everyone in society to make better decisions. Their goal in writing this book is not to bring them more recognition, but it is to ensure that CMP doesn't become an "insiders-only"

club. They seek to increase awareness of this program so that students around the world can become involved in making their communities better places to live. The authors are not just making up these claims—they have actually done the work themselves in the communities. You as the reader are the beneficiaries of the principles, strategies, tools, resources, and lessons that the staff has learned. The Orton Family Foundation wants the program to be a success for all the right reasons. They seek to achieve through CMP the development of tools, methods, and programs that increase citizen involvement in public process, plain and simple.

By working with GIS, GPS, graphics, databases, file management, the Internet, and other computerized tools, students gain valuable, practical workplace skills. However, students pick up more than career skills; they pick up life skills. These include interpersonal skills of leadership, teaching others, negotiation, and working with diversity; resource skills dealing with data collection and analysis, writing, management of time, money, projects, materials, facilities, and human resources; and communications skills that come through working with community leaders, conducting presentations, and working as a team.

Organization of the book

The book is logically organized. CMP is explained in detail, with advice on how to start a project in a local community, and explains who is involved, and why. The book offers practical advice on how to carry out a Community Mapping project from conceptualization to delivery, so that it is sustainable and replicable. The thoroughness of the book is astounding, including practical advice on how to handle administration, technology, and staffing. The book even includes advice on how to start internships for aspiring students to work in their communities, and how to adapt these ideas in a large urban setting. The book's format helps all who are interested to quickly assimilate its ideas.

School district officials, the public, and the state increasingly hold educators accountable for what they are teaching. This book includes assessment tools that will aid in accountability reporting, including an assessment of success and of student learning. CMP also emphasizes sharing results and giving back to the community. Students engaged in CM projects are required to reflect on what they learned.

The case studies are enjoyable to read, and provide ideas that teachers can adapt for their own classrooms. From beetles to eagles, farms to historical buildings, trails to transit systems, auto accidents to groundwater, the case studies illustrate the interdisciplinary nature of this type of work.

Engaging the students

Although the book provides answers to all the details of CMP work, what shines through is that the projects are engaging. The CMP integrates three things that have fascinated people for centuries—maps, the local community, and technology. First, mapmaking (cartography) and the science that uses maps more than any other (geography) have thrived up to the twenty-first century because people have always realized that maps are powerful sources of information. Maps deliver information in paper form that tables and textual information cannot provide. In digital form, maps are even more powerful and versatile, allowing us to explore patterns, linkages, and trends at the community and global scales. At the USGS, I am surrounded by paper and digital maps, and I never tire of sharing them with users all over the world who are as fascinated by maps and our planet as I am.

Second, CM projects are engaging because they involve the local community. Place-based activities have a long tradition in geography and environmental instruction. Often, students do not see the connection between what they are learning in school and what they read and see about their community in the media and through direct observation. Place-based instruction means that the laboratory is in the field, the forest, in neighborhoods, and in the streams of their own city, village, town, and region.

Third, CM projects are engaging because they involve rapidly changing, exciting, spatial technologies that are quickly becoming part of everyday life. GPS and GIS are becoming embedded in cell phones, spreadsheet software, automobiles, and other things that students encounter daily. The spread of this technology into local government organizations is a key ingredient for the success of the Community Mapping Program. Students work with data from the local community that is often provided by local government organizations. Examining their own school on digital aerial photographs and creating three-dimensional views of a local watershed are a few of the many activities that students of all ages find fascinating. These activities encourage students to make connections between human and natural systems, just as they exist in reality.

These three reasons explain why CM projects are engaging, but they also explain why CM projects are successful. In the end, if projects are exciting to community leaders and teachers, but are boring to students, learning stops dead. As one of the students quoted in the book states, "if students had something interesting so that they could see a point to what they were learning, I think there would be a lot more interest and a lot higher grades." A high school student who had been a part of CMP worked with me during a teacher training event that I co-taught with The Orton Family Foundation staff. He enthusiastically put in many hours of his own time during the week to help with technology and training, an example I have witnessed time after time over the past decade with GIS-based, inquiry-based learning.

Students are enthusiastic about these projects because they realize that they can make a difference in their community, and more importantly, they can make a difference right now. The benefits of this type of engagement go far beyond content knowledge and skills. Students feel that they are needed in the community. This can positively influence how they feel about themselves and their own contributions to society.

Making a difference

Making Community Connections advocates starting with identifying the issues of the local community. This is a powerful question for students to think about. *What are the issues in my own community?* I suspect that most students do not even know what the public process is in their community. Through CMP, they will not receive a lecture about the process. Rather, they will participate in it!

Making Community Connections explores the avenues that allow students to contribute to their communities. Too often, the community is suspicious of the activities of students, particularly of teenagers. Society often seems to value our youth solely for their purchasing power. CMP success stories proclaim loud and clear: "You don't have to wait until you graduate or until you can vote in elections before you can make a difference. You can do something this semester."

As the book points out, the students discover that the real world is "messy!" How will they deal with missing data, information that doesn't seem to fit other data, or inaccurate field devices or methods? I believe that the students who truly grapple with the "messy world" through projects like CMP offers are those that we will want to hire for daily, complex decision making in our nature conservancies, our federal agencies such as the USGS and EPA, our state departments of natural resources, and our city and county planning departments. This approach cultivates a network of more informed, more proactive, and responsible citizens and stewards of our lands. That is exactly who we need to solve the complex problems of the twenty-first century.

If CMP takes root in enough communities, one can scarcely imagine the impact on our world. Do we dare to dream that big?

Having been involved in geography education that uses GIS, GPS, and remote sensing technologies for many years, *Making Community Connections* is the first book that I have seen that brings together GIS technology, citizenship, geography, and place-based study. In my opinion, we too often underestimate what students can do and what they can contribute. We are in the twenty-first century—let's give students twenty-first century technology, support, and guidance—we will be amazed at what they can do.

Therefore, *Making Community Connections* is a success story—successful teachers, successful students, successful decision making in our communities. Use it to help you create your own success story.

Preface

In 1999, The Orton Family Foundation supported and oversaw the start-up of the Community Mapping Program (CMP) with simultaneous pilot projects in rural communities of Vermont and Colorado. Ned Swanberg of the Vermont Institute of Natural Science led the Vermont effort and Connie Knapp led the Yampa Valley project in northwest Colorado. Given the different needs and resources initially facing project developers, the Foundation was pleased to see many conceptual similarities arise between them.

This book has been designed to serve as an introduction to the principles, strategies, tools, resources, and lessons learned that contributed to the success of these pioneering efforts—a kind of roadmap for anyone interested in developing a Community Mapping Program (or simply working on one or two free-standing Community Mapping projects). Our success over the past four years attests to the ability of a few motivated people to excite and propel others into action for a common benefit. We believe this model has transferable qualities that can be easily adapted to both rural and urban settings with the appropriate leadership and support.

CMP has benefited greatly from the influence of several emerging educational philosophies and a few key organizations that support education reform, education for sustainability, and the understanding of place. Notably, the state of Vermont has adopted academic standards based on the outcome of the National Forum on Partnerships Supporting Education About the Environment (1994): "Education for Sustainability: An Agenda for Action." Similarly, The Vermont Institute of Natural Science's environmental education programs reflect the sustainability theme, as students are encouraged to explore how our daily decisions affect the natural world.

The Colorado CMP was fortunate to have had the groundwork for place-based, multidisciplinary education previously established by the Yampa Valley Legacy Education Initiative, an Annenberg Rural Challenge (a.k.a. Rural School and Community Trust) beneficiary. Importantly, a 1998 study, conducted by the State Education and Environment Roundtable cooperative called "Closing the Achievement Gap: Using the Environment as an Integrating Context for Learning," quantitatively demonstrated the efficacy of learning through real-world problem solving, and the importance of understanding the interdependence of natural and sociocultural systems. Learning and problem solving through first-hand inquiry into the real world is fundamental to the ongoing success of both pilot projects.

The Community Mapping Program model, on which this book is based, reflects four years of intensive development and documentation, and constant refinement of training, support, implementation, and assessment strategies. Recognizing, for example, that community mapping efforts require more than the development of technical skills and ongoing tech support, we now offer guidelines on how to integrate a variety of other social and life skills for students, including teamwork, public speaking, working with mentors, negotiation, time management, leadership skills, data collection and analysis, writing, and project design and management.

Most of our strategies and guidelines are very flexible and can be easily tailored to meet the needs of other schools and communities, including alternative learning and after-school programs. Even our two pilot projects approached the process of identifying and recruiting educators and community partners differently, for example. Both approaches are presented so that you may use these to determine the most appropriate recruiting plan for your situation.

This book will first introduce you to the Community Mapping Program at the project level. This is often a good place to start because you can focus on completing a well-defined, single project successfully and progress from there as your confidence and support system allow. CM projects generally need dedicated support, at least initially, to coordinate resources, training, planning, and information sharing, and also to provide the technical support and training that allows students and community partners to readily apply the technology without having to first build it from scratch. Such technical and administrative support is often outside the capacities of schools to provide and still accomplish project goals.

We have devoted a whole section of the book to "How to Start a Community Mapping Program." This, we hope, will become the goal of many schools and communities who realize how community–school partnerships can enhance student learning and community connections. The potential of graphic communication tools, like maps, and decision-making tools, like GIS, to foster such community–school relationships is worth considering within the context of your own community dynamics. Both The Orton Family Foundation and the Vermont Institute of Natural Science are available to assist with the design and launching of new Community Mapping Programs.

Training strategies that have evolved substantially over the four years are covered in the next section. Ultimately, new Community Mapping Program sites will want to integrate similar approaches and content into their own local training programs to sustain proficiency among a growing or changing base of participants.

A number of high school students who had been involved in CM projects have helped us take the Community Mapping Program to the next level, namely the school-to-career path. As a result of some very positive experiences with community partners and a new-found passion for GIS by a few students, we have begun facilitating GIS internships and part-time jobs that exemplify the mutual benefits of bringing schools and communities together.

Finally, we have included twelve case studies, six each from the Vermont pilot program and the Yampa Valley CMP in Colorado, to illustrate how the community mapping process played out in the respective states. This is followed by a collection of resources, tools, and references that may come in handy as you embark on community mapping adventures of your own.

"Now more than ever, we need people who think broadly and who understand systems, connections, patterns, and root causes . . . how to think in whole systems, how to find connections, how to ask big questions, and how to separate the trivial from the important."

DAVID W. ORR
EARTH IN MIND: ON EDUCATION, ENVIRONMENT, AND THE HUMAN PROSPECT

How to use this book

Making Community Connections has been created and developed to function as both a kind of template for individual design and as a philosophical guide. It will serve groups of two or three people working with a shoestring budget on a single project, as well as larger groups with more money putting together a program comprised of several projects spread out over a longer period of time. Part 2, "The Community Mapping Project Blueprint," serves both as a general description and as a starting point for teachers considering single projects. Close reading of part 2 and a browse through part 6, "Community Mapping Project Case Studies," is a good way to familiarize yourself with the material. Part 3, "How To Start a Community Mapping Program," covers some of the same material found in part 2, but from the point of view of a coordinator planning larger, longer, and multiple projects.

As you will see from many of our case studies, the school projects are geared towards resources and land use matters in a particular community. We encourage teachers and community members to pursue this direction as it brings the student into contact with local leaders and difficult, multidimensional issues. Such projects inspire and empower these students to get involved in their communities now and in the future. While not trying to dictate the exact content or approach in your project or Program, we do suggest that you try to explore the applications your project may have to community decision making wherever possible. The students love it and they are the ones who will make these decisions in the future!

If you'd like to see more examples, please visit The Orton Family Foundation's Mapping Gallery at *www.communitymap.org.*

Making Community Connections

The Orton Family Foundation Community Mapping Program

"I think it is important for everyone to learn and know about the place they live. Without that knowledge, there would be no community, because people would have no common ground to stand on."

A VERMONT STUDENT

Part 1

Introduction

The Community Mapping
Program (CMP) was developed
as a grassroots effort, by and
for a few rural communities
in Colorado and Vermont. The
Community Mapping (CM) vision,
methodologies, and processes
presented here were developed and
fine-tuned over the years by the
people who put them into practice.

The Community Mapping Program

The Community Mapping Program is an open-ended, dynamic, and broadly inclusive way of bringing students, teachers, and other members of a community together to better understand the places in which they live, the social and political issues affecting those places, and means by which those issues might be best addressed. K–12 students learn how to use mapping and decision-making tools, such as geographic information systems (GIS), in collaboration with local community organizations bringing otherwise unavailable or overlooked resources to bear on projects and issues of mutual concern. Last but not least, Community Mapping projects support teachers in meeting educational standards and other academic goals.

Community Mapping projects are as varied as the partners who develop them.

Imagine how many issues and problems a wildlife agency, a national historical park, a planning commission, and an ambulance service face every day. Sometimes organizations as diverse as these will come together over common issues, managing elk and bears, for example, in a ski area. Generally, when a teacher expresses an interest in certain topics and disciplines, a community partner can readily provide authentic issues that address specific curricular goals, and a mapping component can be easily inserted. Importantly, the CMP promotes students' understanding of spatial relationships with or without the aid of GIS technology. An activity as simple and straightforward as marking on an area map the locations of the studios of local artists or the homes of elder residents who have contributed stories to an

Bear sightings were analyzed by a three-person team: student, teacher, and a Division of Wildlife mentor. Data was collected with a GPS unit and displayed via a GIS.

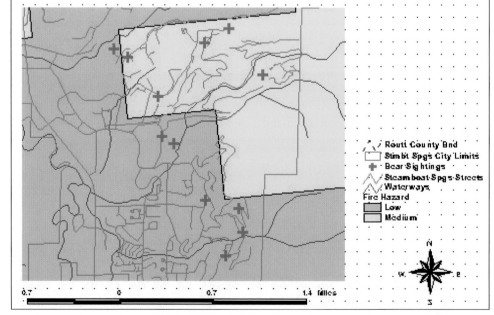

oral history project can shed new light on the culture and heritage of a community, cultivate a sense of place, and open new doors for further study.

As the number of Community Mapping projects increased and diverse experiences accrued, a number of common elements emerged that we have summarized in the form of six guiding principles. The commitment of schools and community partners to addressing them is fundamental to the success of both full-scale Community Mapping Programs and individual Community Mapping projects.

- Community needs
- Connections and continuity
- Place-based learning
- Visualization and technology
- Sharing results
- Reflection and assessment

While these principles primarily reflect the dynamic nature of school–community partnerships, they are also suggestive of how technology cannot stand alone in its application to problem solving in the real world. Mapping technologies, in particular, provide powerful and relatively easy-to-use information management and graphic communication tools, but what's most important—and exciting—about these technologies is the way they enhance understanding. In other words, it's not the vast amount of data a program can tap into, or the colorful map that the software can manufacture for display—it's the content and what can be learned from that data and that display that matters. Imagine how effective it would be to show the migration of a local river channel over time by overlaying maps of the riverbed from different years. Could these maps be used to forecast future movements or the loss of a valued resource? It is in such questions that technology and the needs of a community come together.

Photos from the field and digital elevation maps also figured in the bear-sighting project.

Guiding principles

Community needs

Through collaboration, local community organizations and schools examine, define, and address real needs from a local perspective. Working simultaneously through the leadership and public mission of the community organization and the education goals and standards of the school, a Community Mapping project works to create shared experiences, a language of place, and useful products that address the expressed needs of the community.

Connections and continuity

Community Mapping projects encourage people of all ages and skills to work together to identify, understand, value, and enhance the human and natural systems that will sustain and build local—and eventually, global—communities. Projects connect people to one another and to the social, economic, educational, and ecological threads of their communities through investigations that create greater understanding, relevant curricula, and products useful to the communities.

Placed-based learning

Community Mapping projects use questions of place to provoke and integrate student learning. By connecting real community issues with educational standards through a hands-on, multidisciplinary inquiry process, the students gain broad understanding of the fabric of where they live and how to act powerfully in their community. Mapping and decision-making tools such as geographic information systems (GIS) work most effectively when educators and community mentors guide and support the students as active learners addressing real issues.

Visualization and technology

The Orton Family Foundation's Community Mapping Program uses technology to enhance communication, learning, and informed decision making among students, educators, community members, and organizations. Visualization and information management tools, such as GIS mapping and planning software, databases, and the Internet support successful collaborations in rural communities.

Sharing results

Community Mapping projects build new insights and enduring connections in communities when they are actively shared across boundaries. Public display and forums enhance the value of the projects, build student confidence, promote civic participation, and foster stronger community–school relationships.

Reflection and assessment

The Community Mapping Program strives to understand its key role: bringing schools and communities together to address their mutual needs and build an enduring future. Using a variety of assessment methods and forums, it assesses its work from the level of student learning to that of systemic change in schools and communities. From this ongoing programmatic process of reflection and adaptation, we are able to support the real and changing needs of our rural communities.

Four experiences in a Community Mapping project

A Community Mapping project involves three key local groups—students, educators, and a community partner. Initially, the project may also involve a fourth entity, the CMP staff, working closely with a project team to plan and implement the project.

As projects get underway and the processes of community assessment, problem solving, and spatial expression are committed to, the responsibilities of leadership will become collaborative in nature, with all three groups participating equally. Participants outside the core group can be recruited as needed, since the initiation of a Community Mapping project is often the first attempt school–community collaboration; not only have needs yet to be identified and connections made—the means of making those choices and connections must be devised and tried. Projects at this stage also typically lack ready access to dynamic map resources, decision-making tools, and other spatial tools (global positioning system equipment, for example), making specific kinds of outreach inevitable.

Depending on local leadership and conditions, a Community Mapping project creates opportunity for school–community dialogue, self-assessment, problem identification, resource identification, training, and so on, as outlined in the diagram. Each of the four groups supports the success of the project in different ways and at different times. A project starts small and builds on success.

A completed project identifies additional community needs and increases the community's capacity to address them.

Youth provide a capacity to learn—as students, as members of the community, and as increasingly powerful participants in community life.

Students are the members of the community who are encouraged to apply new skills, reflect on new knowledge, conduct investigations, and contribute new insights about local conditions and systems in the light of global conditions

Community Continues Work

Final Community Discussion
Final Products

Draft Products

Educators
Link ideas & needs
Enable action
Guide learning

Public Forums
Reiteration
Analysis
Field Work

Community Mapping Program Staff
Nurture local capacity
Provide tools
Provide support
Provide training

Skills Development
Team Development
Training and Tools Acquisition

Students
Relevant learning
Apply new skills
Community participation
Gain confidence

Community Partner
Mentors & role models
Subject matter experts
Link to real issues
Public mission

Standards/Assessment Planning
Product ID/ Timeline Establishment
Project Planning
Resource Identification

Community Assessment

Growing A Community Mapping Project

This tree illustrates a Community Mapping project. The project begins with a seed on the local soil.

and tools of understanding. Their investments in the project—the collaboration, the assessment, the problem identification, functioning local systems, and the future—are all authentic incentives for the students and critical for community success.

Educators enable students to try new skills, discover new knowledge, attempt original inquiry, engage in collaboration, develop analyses, and articulate insights. The work of educators frame and reinforce this learning through good organization and providing real-world feedback for the students' investigative efforts. The educators enable the students to act powerfully and responsibly in their work while also meeting the critical needs, expectations, and deadlines of the community partner.

Educators are critical as doorkeepers, and as adults capable of enabling skill and resource acquisition. The lifelong learning behaviors and experiences that schools can provide are valuable for the community as a whole. Their enabling work as educators needs to be matched by the special leadership of a community organization that can bring in history, support, and vision.

The community partner works in partnership with the school or after-school program (educators, students, and administration) to provide a critical leadership component and to mobilize resources. The community organization has a public mission and goals, organizational tools for communication and resource identification, and an understanding of how their organizational needs relate to those of the community. The community organization also has a clear need for the work of the project: the building of local school and community capacity and the new knowledge or products that will address the mission of the organization as well as the long-term success of the community.

The community partner is also invited into the process at multiple points. The project does not need to be created entirely by young people; it needs to be the best work of the community. This is a goal that will satisfy all parties concerned, this time and next time and the time after that.

CMP staff plays a key role by supplying what is missing but critically needed. The success of a project may be limited by one or many elements: mutual needs, catalyst, skills, models, data, technology, support, and reinforcement. The role of CMP staff is to act adequately but minimally to enable a successful project and promote momentum and capacity for further community self-directed action.

The CMP staff is keen to see the initiation of community project self-organization and continuity. Over time, the training, shared experiences, new skills, and other resources will enable the local mapping project groups to work with increasing interdependence, articulate a distinctive vision connected to place, identify choice paths to the future, and engage with the best of the world's insights and problem-solving tools.

Community–school relationships may not necessarily or inherently develop in a natural manner, and the team members will never have adequate time to anticipate and coordinate all the details. Training, good communication, and old-fashioned experience can eventually lead to more independently led projects, but we found that the most effective approach featured dedicated outside leadership and support.

Along the tree trunk (page 5) are some of the discrete actions, processes, and notable contributions that each group may engage in, either independently or collectively, as a Community Mapping project evolves.

Ideally students, educators, and the community partner are involved end-to-end: from project conception to final assessment. Their roles may shift throughout the life of the project, with students sometimes taking on a contractor role or apprentice and the community partner taking on that of both a student of the process and mentor of the students.

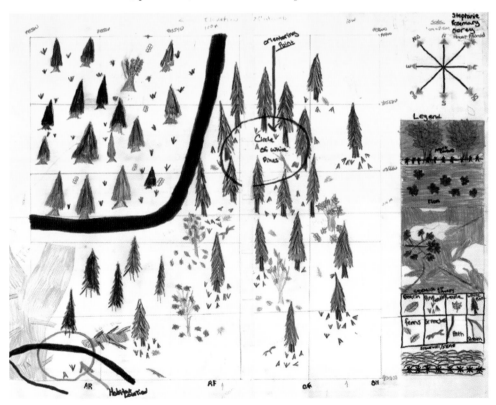

A Community Mapping project need not incorporate the latest technology. Hand-drawn maps can tell convincing stories, too.

What are Community Mapping projects?

Community Mapping projects are (or at least can be) the foundation of community–school cooperation. This is where the work gets done; all participants gain greater knowledge and appreciation of each other, their respective needs and talents, and ultimately the issues under investigation. A CM project is multifaceted because it involves not only a master plan of execution, but also the ongoing and coordinated sharing of all types of resources, from subject matter experts to equipment, software, and data, to information.

A project also demands constant communication between participants—the educators, community mentors, and students. Providing regular feedback to students in the form of formative assessments from both the educators and community mentors, throughout the development, implementation, and delivery of a project, is paramount to staying on track and meeting project goals. If a community partner is expecting a comprehensive mapping product for a public meeting and a student turns in mediocre "C" work the day before the meeting, who is to blame and how will the students and partner feel about this outcome?

Sometimes the community partner may be more interested in the process of public education than in the actual products generated, so it is important for the educators to understand this from the beginning. Two atmospheric scientists in Colorado led precipitation-monitoring projects as a way to promote an understanding of how climate affects us—the economics of local agriculture and ski resort industries are certainly very dependent on weather patterns. Similarly, a wildlife manager involved students in the drafting of a wildlife area management plan as a way to draw in public participation, not only concerning the wildlife area at issue, but to also expand the public's awareness of how important their input can be in shaping public lands management strategies.

As in any successful partnership, the outcomes—both tangible and intangible—benefit all parties. In the case of CM projects, the students, teachers, and community partner all benefit from the process and products involved. Hence, it is critical that respective needs,

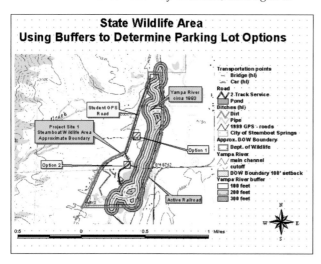

CM projects bring people from different parts of a community together to address issues of mutual concern.

"We need to develop in students the capacity to be stewards of their place. This can be done through changing the way in which education is conducted. This change needs to include more hands-on, real-life experiences."

DAVID W. ORR
EARTH IN MIND: ON EDUCATION, ENVIRONMENT, AND THE HUMAN PROSPECT

expectations, and ultimate benefits be articulated at the outset of each project and agreement reached about a feasible timeline and scope of work. While we found that the excitement of introducing technology—such as mapping and GIS—may initially ignite a new school–community relationship, mutual needs must drive the technology and not the other way around.

Educators and community members alike are quick to point out that GIS must be applied as a tool and not as the main focus of a mutual project. Reinhold Friebertshauser, cofounder of the Chagrin Institute and teacher at University School in Ohio, summarized this concept best in his article published in *GEO Info Systems* (April 1997) called "Higher Learning: GIS in Nontraditional Curriculums":

We began our journey at the University School by asking the question, "How do we get GIS into our curriculum?" We now believe that the question itself led us down a dead end. When we began asking, "How can we, as K-12 teachers and students, use GIS technology?" that dead end opened into a world of broad horizons. We are no longer concerned about GIS being formally incorporated in the curriculum. Rather, something far more profound will happen if we succeed at our goals. Individual teachers and students will sneak GIS technology into the curriculum because they are using it elsewhere. And they will do it in ways that work for them.

Some of us assumed in the beginning that engaging students in the initial phases of project selection and design would ensure more enthusiastic buy-in and ownership. While this may be true, we also discovered that project design work was far more involved than could be feasibly done by students during the school year on top of satisfactorily completing a project. We found it was more critical to engage students in the processes of discovery and the application of new skills as quickly as possible. This generally means that the educators, community partners, and CMP staff must accomplish much of the planning and preparation prior to engaging the students. Alternatively, encouraging students to identify teams and lead tasks can achieve a similar effect.

Determining the capabilities of students is also important to defining the complexity of CM projects and committing to specific outcomes. This will be addressed in more detail in subsequent sections. However, David Sobel's research is worth recognizing here, as his findings have profoundly influenced the evolution of our model in the K–12 arena. We first introduced mapping and GIS technologies at the middle and high school levels and subsequently expanded project involvement to the lower grades. Certainly a plausible alternative approach might have

elementary teachers initiating simple mapping projects that prepare students for the more technical road ahead and expanding upward. If you consider that one educational project goal might be to increase students' understanding of spatial relationships, it is easy to see how CM projects might address this in the lower grade levels if basic mapping skills and manual maps were substituted for GIS technology.

Typically, CM projects are characterized by the study of place, which cultivates a deeper, more complex, and ultimately more satisfying sense of place among all those affected by the experience—students, teachers, parents, citizens, community leaders, and often community visitors. How better to study the heritage, culture, ecology, and economics of a place than to immerse oneself directly in it? CM projects are predicated on such an approach—getting students out of the classroom and into their community to study real issues first-hand and to apply new problem-solving tools and skills in the process of discovery. The Yampa Valley Legacy Education Initiative and similar programs call this place-based education, although it is also often referred to as problem-based, project-based, or inquiry-based education.

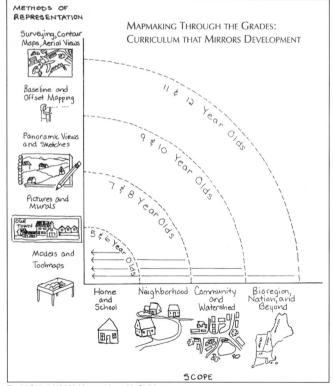

David Sobel (1998) *Mapmaking with Children*

Effective ways of teaching and using the many and various technologies now available to students of all ages is an important part of CM training.

"We have a vision, but not the time or resources to build it. Kids know how to turn our vision into reality. That's what makes it a partnership."

JAY MUHME
FIRE MARSHALL, STEAMBOAT SPRINGS FIRE PREVENTION DIVISION

Part 2

The Community Mapping Project Blueprint

Project ideas, issues, and topics may come from a variety of sources. The key is to identify people in the community who share common interests with you and then get together to explore possibilities. During initial brainstorming sessions, it is important to look for spatial and temporal relationships that might be best expressed graphically through some form of map, either handmade or with a GIS. Maps are unlimited in their potential to enhance understanding in most every discipline, from science, business, and math to history, art, and the languages.

Mobilizing a collaborative process

The following scenarios illustrate how a Community Mapping project might begin.

Scenario 1:
A community member has project ideas
A conservation organization that manages a local land parcel was hoping to recruit volunteers to help out with a number of projects including marking and interpreting a nature trail; locating ditches, wells, and streams on a map; monitoring river bank erosion; and planting willows along erosion-prone sections of the river. A middle school science teacher who volunteers for the organization proposed that her students could tackle one or two of these opportunities as part of their natural environment class. The organization suggested that that data could be incorporated into a GIS as a basis for tracking and managing the parcel's resources and that the students could easily learn how to use GPS units to collect the data. An agreement was reached to have the students map the hydrologic features of the parcel using GPS and GIS technology, followed by a willow-planting field trip and celebration picnic. More data could be added to the GIS base map over time, eventually yielding a dynamic management tool for use by the organization and more project possibilities for students.

Scenario 2:
An educator has an interest in local heritage
An english teacher wanted his students to read and critique local material, not only to satisfy academic reading standards, but to also gain an appreciation of the local culture and heritage. The teacher contacted the library and a writers club to discover what was available and learned that quite a few oral histories had been recently donated to the museum. The museum director was interested in having the oral histories organized according to content, period, and other criteria, and also in locating the residences of the oral historians and any referenced landmarks on maps. The museum director suggested that students could collect exact locations of these landmarks using GPS units and then transfer the points into a GIS. The english teacher took an interdisciplinary approach and asked a geography teacher to tackle the mapping portion of the museum's project while his class focused on the extracting relevant content from the histories. In this scenario, the community partner and educators found a way to integrate a mapping component into a project, which enhanced the final product with meaningful graphics.

The project mobilization phase can be the most creative and least restrictive process involved in undertaking a Community Mapping project. Brainstorming the range of possibilities generally starts out as a nonjudgmental process that encourages input from all interested representatives. Community members, educators, or students can initiate the process of developing project ideas. The best time to do this is well in advance of the investigation and prior to sending representatives to CM training. The project mobilization phase should focus primarily on identifying and organizing the mutual interests of potential community partners and educators who are willing to explore collaborative possibilities involving youth. Engaging youth in the entire process is strongly recommended and represents the ideal approach, but is often impractical at these very early stages.

Project coordination group

As a newly CM-trained educator or educator team, consider initially assembling a cross section of interested individuals from the community and your school to discuss one or more CM project themes that would fit into your academic goals for a semester or the school year. Certain invitees should come immediately to mind. Besides community experts and other educators involved in the discipline(s) of interest, your invitation list might also include city and county managers and other appropriate government agency representatives. Organizations with resources that may be needed to carry out the project should all be invited to participate in the initial coordination meeting.

If you already have a community partner lined up and a general project idea in mind, the process of identifying potential partners and key issues through a project coordination group may not be necessary. Schools and youth groups with little previous experience working with community organizations, however, would benefit from the interactions involved and the level of community awareness generated by a collaborative approach to developing CM project ideas.

The following approach is recommended at the start of a new Community Mapping project, primarily for political reasons, but also to ensure that widespread interest is ready to follow and support the ensuing efforts. Starting at the project level may naturally lead to the formation of a CMP as one project grows into many over time. Of course, at the CMP level, a dedicated CMP staff would facilitate the mobilization process across all projects. The project mobilization approach starts the process out at the broadest possible extent within a selected theme to avoid excluding any key interests, resources, and guidance.

Subsequent conceptualization and planning activities will narrow the scope of the project to match essential needs with available resources, schedules, and student capabilities.

In anticipation of attending CM training together, a high school geography teacher and math teacher convened a project coordination meeting around a theme of mutual interest:

MOBILIZING A COMMUNITY MAPPING PROJECT		
	ACTION	**EXAMPLE**
1	Identify theme of interest	*Highway motor vehicle accidents and traffic issues*
2	Identify coordination group ASK: 　Who might care? 　Who might help?	*City and county directors of emergency management services* *Local ambulance service representatives* *City and county law enforcement reps (police and fire)* *Other high school geography teachers* *Other high school math teachers* *High school principal* *High school curriculum development coordinator* *High school technology coordinator* *High school school-to-career coordinator* *High school guidance counselor* *City and county GIS specialists (to advise on data availability)* *Hospital spokesperson* *Related nonprofit organization representatives* *Citizens affected by past accidents* *Businesses affected by traffic issues* *Local newspaper reporter (to further publicize the initiative)*
3	Hold coordination meeting PURPOSE: 　Recruit support 　Expand awareness 　Develop common language 　Identify mutual benefits	*Brainstorm purpose and benefits of community–school partnership* *Brainstorm potential broad project ideas concerning accidents and traffic issues* *Narrow the list of specific project ideas—define key questions* *Brainstorm mapping products and practice exercises* *Brainstorm academic disciplines that can be integrated* *Educate community members on academic standards and goals* *Educate school administrators and educators on community needs* *Identify who would form core project team—teachers, classes, community members, and organizations* *Nominate potential community mentor to work with and guide students* *Identify who would provide ongoing support and data as needed*
4	Turn issue into project	*Agree on key issues or questions to investigate* *Identify individuals who will conceptualize and plan the project* *Agree to move forward with a core project team that will conceptualize and plan the project in more detail*

SUGGESTED COMMUNITY ROLES AND RESPONSIBILITIES

Link students and communities through local projects
Be a mentor: Take on the roles of educator and mentor when working with the students.
Be flexible and open to students' perspectives: Help students examine root cause(s) of issues and support their questions of *Why?* and finally *What if?*
Lead students to successful completion of project objectives: Several small successes are better than one huge failure.
Provide students with a link to the real world
Demonstrate the value of products by using them: Validate product need.
Become students of this pilot project approach: Adopt the project goals and curriculum objectives.

PROJECT GOALS AT-A-GLANCE

- Community-based projects integrated into existing curricula
- Students pursue and help develop projects of interest
- Tangible products
- Public presentation of products and results
- Web site access to project data, map gallery, communications hub, curriculum framework model, project documentation

- Approach: Interdisciplinary, place-based, inquiry-based
- School–community relationships (mentoring and collaboration)
- Transferable curriculum
- Products meaningful to the community
- Local issues/local needs

The Colorado project coordination group also discussed the merits of tailoring CM investigations to achieve the following goals: 1) establish a framework for an inquiry-based and place-based approach to project design, 2) reinforce the concepts of education for sustainability and sense of place, and 3) demonstrate how mapping technologies can be applied to many interdisciplinary topics and issues. This exercise fosters the free flow of ideas, cooperation among participants, and widespread ownership of the CM project objectives. Importantly, Community Mapping projects can instigate data sharing among agencies with no prior history of cooperating at this level.

It is good practice to think small and simple during the project mobilization phase and to ultimately seek appropriate help in assessing whether your project ideas are, in fact, small and simple. Understanding GIS capabilities, how to introduce new technical skills to students and the basics of project management can lead to realistic projects and feasible timelines. This constitutes the core of CM training. Another good practice to adopt early on is to consider GIS purely as a tool to more effectively communicate information about an issue through visual means.

BRAINSTORMING MAP THEMES

Cemeteries: Birthdays, death dates, headstone types, tie the deceased back to their homesteads, war veterans, link between birth and death dates, what kind of info can you find?, epitaphs, age at death, family groups, matrilineal lines, socioeconomic and racial information, and so forth.

Watersheds: Water quality, agricultural lands, plants, industries, well sites, changing water sources.

Literature: Where stories originated, author locations, map stories, differences between fiction and reality, ghost sitings and stories.

Historical landmarks and buildings: Architectural types, significance, dates, building materials, changes in architecture, relationship to each other and the changing town, cellar holes, ownership transfer, ecological history.

Trails: Hiking, horse, foot, cycle, snowmobile, development dates, support services, changes from road to trail and vice versa, railroads.

Pets and animals: Animal types, distribution, movement patterns, keeping track, roadkill, wildlife, corridor tracking.

Dumping patterns: Locations, materials found, timeline of events, ownership.

Archaeology: Depth, location, item, size, significance, Neolithic sites, petroglyphs.

Natural resources: Minerals, soils, water, best solar locations.

Miscellaneous: Malls, shops, hangouts, safe places, recreation areas, houses, homes, hunting, ancestral.

BRAINSTORMING MAPPING EXERCISES

- Compass work
- Orienteering
- Hand draw maps then convert to GIS
- 3–D modeling
- Contrast scale vs. relationship maps
- Map the same site from different perspectives
- Map animal tracks and routes in the snow
- Experiment with artistic input
- Experiment with different tourism themes
- GPS data collection—map school grounds
- Combine existing GIS data with new data
- Download data from the Internet
- Search the Internet for related maps and data
- Apply different map projections to local map

BRAINSTORMING MAPPING PRODUCTS

- Sounds, smells, senses, and so on
- Contour maps
- Topographic maps locating specific features
- Watershed or drainage maps
- Demographics
- Community values
- Tourist maps
- Literary map of authors
- Cross-section maps
- Camping and hiking maps
- Architectural maps
- Traffic and transportation maps
- Maps showing spatial trends
- Maps showing temporal trends

BRAINSTORMING COMMUNITY BENEFITS

- Products of value contributed
- Public awareness of issues
- Public participation in issue resolution
- Access to academic resources
- Interorganizational cooperation
- Turn students into involved citizens
- Turn parents into involved citizens
- GIS product as tool to manage resources
- Project may attract budget support

Communities and community partners realize greater value than just the products generated

BRAINSTORMING EDUCATOR FEARS

- Possibility to be overwhelming
- May be overwhelmed with technology
- Project may not get finished
- Feeling of being unprepared
- May revert to old ways of doing things
- May require more hours
- Fear of unknown
- Challenge of change
- Reality factor will hit

Identify hopes and fears during project mobilization

BRAINSTORMING EDUCATOR HOPES

- Provide authentic experiences for students
- Generate real applications
- Integrate technology into classroom and field
- Rewarding experience
- Enhance curricula and student learning
- Students are creative within the community
- Teachers can work together
- Generate meaning for students
- Promote student involvement
- Promote place-based education
- Promote education for sustainability
- Introduce transferable skills
- Exposure to professionals and career choices

Address hopes and fears head on during project conceptualization and planning

Conceptualization and planning

The conceptualization and planning phase is generally the most crucial part of carrying out a Community Mapping project because this is when goals are set and products defined. If compelling academic and community needs are not clearly articulated at the outset, for example, the project may not ultimately address the right ones. Similarly, if the goals and products turn out to be too ambitious or divisive, the project will fail to meet expectations. In this section we will examine a number of ways to define realistic scopes of work for CM projects, with the common objective of keeping projects small and simple.

Teachers, students, community members, and local initiatives are all great sources of CM project ideas. The CM project conceptualization process assumes that appropriate "real" issues can be readily identified and either scoped down or broken into multiple projects. Alternatively, it is also quite appropriate to back up a step and lead students and community representatives through the process of identifying priority issues with the aid of skilled facilitators. Time permitting, this can actually be a valuable learning experience for students and community members who have not gone through this type of exercise.

Readiness and commitment

The conceptualization and planning phase involves collecting a lot of initial information to help assess both the level of readiness to tackle a specific project and the level of commitment each team member has toward making this collaborative effort a success. This information can come together in a variety of ways. One way is through a structured application process instigated by a request for proposals from an authorized Community Mapping training center, such as the Vermont Institute of Natural Science, that encourages project teams to mobilize around an issue or question early on and then participate in CM training to further define the project and to learn the necessary skills. If school principals and technology coordinators are required to complete certain parts of the application, this not only adds to the information base, but also serves to increase the awareness and support of school administrators. In this structured approach, project members make a commitment to pursue a generally defined project and then participate in CM training, project planning, and curriculum development work to further define and implement the project. Modest funding incentives may be offered to participating educators for training and subsequent project implementation, including follow-up support by the CM training team if desired (see sample budget in the appendix).

The more informal project conceptualization approach employs a "try it, you'll like it" process of training educators prior to seeking a commitment from any of the other team members. Educators and potential community partners still explore conceptual project ideas prior to CM training—because training is most effective when participants come with at least a broad project idea in mind—but no commitments are made until after the training. This informal strategy, exercised by authorized CM training centers like The Orton Family Foundation's Colorado CMP, still requires that community members complete Project Description Forms and that teachers fill out Educator Needs Forms (see appendix) to clarify respective needs prior to CM training. These forms are exchanged or shared among all members of the project team as a basis for conceptualizing a feasible project design. In the informal approach, the commitment to participate in a CM project is made after training and only when the entire team understands what will be required to carry out the project and is ready to forge ahead together. Follow-up support may not be necessary after CM training, given the replicable nature of the skills taught, emphasis on designing small and simple projects, and opportunities for educators to consult with instructors throughout the CM training.

In both the structured and informal project conceptualization approaches, educator teams attend CM training to learn how to effectively design, implement, and deliver CM projects with their community partners—projects that are based on their working knowledge of GIS and solid project management skills that meet respective needs and are consistent with available resources.

Information gathering

Both the structured application process and the informal conceptualization process accomplish initial information-gathering objectives that are vital to the design of a viable, successful project. These objectives, outlined in the table on the next page, illustrate the range of tasks and limitations that community members and educators must address in order to lay a solid foundation for project planning and design. Where missing resources are identified, the project team may decide to track these down locally or construct alternative or interim measures to keep an acceptable form of the project moving forward. This stage of the conceptualization process may also be referred to as the "Who, Why, What, Where, When, and How" stage of project development.

PROJECT DESIGN OBJECTIVES	EXAMPLES
1 Identify specific academic needs	Academic standards, curriculum objectives
2 Identify specific community needs	Issues, questions, products, product quality, deadlines
3 Identify available resources	Time, budget, people*, equipment, software, data, venues
4 Identify missing resources	Time, budget, people*, equipment, software, data, venues
5 Identify necessary skills	GIS/GPS, mapping, data collection, data analysis, research, speaking, writing, time management, teamwork, leadership, and so forth
6 Define community benefits	GIS/map products, Web page, kiosk, citizen involvement, presentations, resource monitoring, data collection, data archival, and so forth
7 Define academic benefits	Academic standards, student achievement, student confidence
8 Define the mapping component	Hand-drawn maps, field data collection/mapping, GPS/GIS, data analysis, final presentation
9 Clarify shared goals, vision, and desired outcomes	Apply new skills to create products that help community leaders make better decisions, keep constituents better informed, and helps students learn specific academic and life skills
10 Set interim and final deadlines	Community input, student work, student assessments, final products
11 Incorporate time for lessons and skills development into schedule	GIS/GPS training and warm-up activities, presentation rehearsals, data collection protocol, data analysis instruction, and so forth
12 Define key roles	Community mentor, educators, students, CMP staff, technology coordinators, other experts
13 Confirm commitment of community mentor	Hours per month, types of support, regular feedback to students, share experiences and results
14 Confirm commitment of educators	Class time, field trips, skills training, student assessment, share experiences and results

* People resources may include: teachers, students, technology coordinators, community mentors, subject matter experts, GIS/GPS specialists, parents, volunteers, service/resource providers, business owners, or technical, managerial, or service professionals, and so on.

Clarification of roles

Clarifying the principle roles of each member on a CM project team is an essential brainstorming exercise during project conceptualization meetings and discussions of commitment. The table that follows resulted from a discussion of roles for a Colorado-based CM project.

EDUCATORS
- Primary link to students
- Work together for interdisciplinary approach
- Colead project with community mentor
- Develop and implement curriculum
- Generate ideas for sustainability
- *Spark plugs* of motivation for student learning and achievement
- Facilitate ongoing communications among entire project team
- Conduct regular assessments of student work and solicit input from community mentor
- Introduce mapping technologies to students *within acknowledged technical capacity and comfort levels,* drawing on outside support as available.

STUDENTS
- Benefactors
- Generators
- Choose projects or tasks of interest
- Present project results to community
- Investigators, explorers, and inquirers
- Data collectors
- Learn and apply new technical and life skills
- Develop new perspectives
- Team players
- Professional apprentices

COMMUNITY PARTNERS (project host and mentor, also subject-matter experts for leading specific tasks)
- Link students with community and the real world
- Facilitate mentoring (i.e., take on the roles of educator and mentor when working with students)
- Be flexible and open to student perspectives (i.e., help students examine root cause(s) of issues and support their questions of *why?* and finally, *what if?*)
- Lead students to successful completion of project objectives
- Demonstrate value of products by using them
- Teach students practical skills and professional ethics; explain related career opportunities
- Have a real and discrete need that the student work will address

Project design

Once the initial information has been gathered, it must next be assimilated into a schedule and a project design that is amenable to all team members who have committed to contributing to or carrying out the project. The diagrams on the next page illustrate how a CM project may be viewed at the task level by educators and by students. The diagrams are provided as tools to facilitate ongoing school–community communication and understanding, including the development of a common language and mutual objectives.

The education component

The nature, design, and scope of CM projects are highly dependent on how much time educators, students, and community members feel they will have to plan and carry them out. Some educators may only be able to devote eight class periods over a six-week time period to the project, or less. *How long are your class periods? How much can you accomplish in fifty minutes, or ninety minutes? Do you have the support of your school principal to schedule several half-day field trips, including hiring substitute teachers and arranging transportation to the sites?* We have found that, with adequate notice and encouragement, many principals and school administrators enjoy participating in field efforts alongside the students. Their direct observation of effective learning opportunities in action can only serve to amplify their support of your CM project and their own appreciation of student capabilities.

Available time can be the most critical resource in determining what can feasibly be accomplished and also meet the respective needs and mutual interests of all team members. Timing is also important, as your community partner may only be able to focus on a project during the winter months when fieldwork may be difficult or impossible. How might these parameters affect the design of your project? If new data cannot be collected, could students work with existing data instead? Could another community expert supervise student data collection at another time of the year? Would either the community goals or academic objectives be compromised if fieldwork and data collection were eliminated? Time commitments must be made relatively early in the project design process, as these will directly affect the final nature and outcome of the project.

AT THE EDUCATOR LEVEL

Project: Create NPS Pollution Index for a watershed
Mercator Middle School, Someplace, USA

Implementation Processes

Educators receive needs-specific training
- Summer workshops
- Mentor with partner organization
- Independent research and education

Educators develop curriculum for the unit
- Investigate standards
- Block out learning units
- Develop unit goals
- Work with partner to maximize opportunities
- Schedule
- Develop budget
- Assessment criteria

Instructional phase
- Educator teaches the components/steps to the students to develop a skill set and context
- Students become familiar with tech tools

Product phase
- Students and educators refine the project process and conceptualize a revised final product/outcome
- Students do work/research related to final product/outcomes

Presentation phase
- Students pull the pieces together for the presentation of results
- Partner facilitates/mentors/helps

Assessment phase
- Students, educators, partners review the strengths and weaknesses of the project

TASK FLOW

Partners   *Teachers*

CM PROJECT

Students ➤

SYNTHESIS AND MERGING PROCESSES

OUTCOME / PRODUCT / RESULTS

Organizational Processes

School–community structure
Teacher contracts
Student discipline issues
Conflict resolution
Authentication/validation
Resource constraints
Ideology constraints

This project is past the concept stage; the educators and partners have signed on to it.

Embedded within the school's task to create the pollution index for a watershed are the curriculum objectives for educators.

AT THE STUDENT LEVEL

Project: Create NPS Pollution Index for a watershed
Mercator Middle School, Someplace, USA

Implementation Processes

TASK FLOW

Project design

Team building

Skills and knowledge enhancement

Research and field work

Data compilation and analyzation

Product assembly

Presentation

Assessment

Partners   *Teachers*

CM PROJECT

Students ➤

SYNTHESIS AND MERGING PROCESSES

OUTCOME / PRODUCT / RESULTS

Organizational Processes

Access to tools

Classroom environment

Access to information

Conflict resolution

Resource allocation

Group dynamics

Disruptions and discipline

Motivational factors

This project is past the concept stage; the educators and partners have signed on to it.

Embedded within the school's task to create the pollution index for a watershed are the roles of the participants, educators, teachers, and students.

The first outline below depicts a schedule, or timeline, for a CM project that was restricted to eight class periods over four weeks, plus a public presentation. Class periods were generally forty-five minutes, but two were extended to ninety minutes to accommodate fieldwork. In this project, the community partner engaged other specialists to help broaden high school students' understanding of how climate variables are measured and tracked and ultimately how climate affects us—our economy, recreation, and lifestyles.

The next timeline reflects a much longer and complex project involving data collection, use of GPS and GIS, and developing a final brochure layout for publication.

CLIMATE MAPPING PROJECT

Class #1	What are the sources of historical and current climate measurements?
Class #2	What is GIS and how is it used to map precipitation and other climate data?
Class #3	How do we use hand contouring to analyze the distribution of snowfall?
Field Trip	GPS Orienteering: How has the location of climate stations changed this century?
Class #5	What techniques are used to enter snowfall data into an ESRI® ArcView® database?
Museum Visit	In what ways has climatology influenced our local history?
Class #7	Writing Assignment: How would you use GIS in a community project?
Class #8	Computer Training: What techniques are used for water resources monitoring?
Storyboard Presentation	What did we learn from the Climate Mapping project?

STATE PARKS WILDLIFE BROCHURE PROJECT

Preliminary 2000–2001 Timeline

Thursday	Sept. 21		Orientation field trip: Bus trip along the adopted stretch of the Yampa River
Friday	Sept. 29	Due Date	First batch of wildlife photos to State Parks
Friday	Dec. 15	Due Date	Last batch of wildlife photos, artwork, and maps to instructor
	January	Start	Graphics screening and selection, design layout, writing narratives, selecting map locations to highlight and key to an index, and so on
Tuesday	Jan. 30	Due Date	Draft mark-up, graphics, design layout, written narratives and captions, map locations to highlight and index key, and so on
	Feb.–March	Review Period	With State Parks, conduct several cycles of brochure review, improvement, and enhancement
Friday	April 13	Due Date	Camera-ready brochure to State Parks for printing

NOTE: More field trips and milestones will be scheduled as project design progresses

The CMP addresses the time issue by providing educator training and project design consultation during the summer months. The instruction addresses curriculum development and provides time to do it in a facilitated group or project team setting. Other summer training topics focus on how to introduce a new technology to students, apply fundamental project management principles and build effective community–school relationships that maximize the impact on student learning, achievement and self-esteem. Equally important is the topic of how much GIS should CM-trained educators plan to teach students and build into a CM project. The appropriate answer is not only limited by available class time and access to computers, but by both the technical competency and post-training confidence of the responsible educator and the

students' demonstrated proficiency with computers and technology in general. Given adequate time to bring students up to speed on the prerequisite technical skills, CM projects may ultimately serve as a catalyst in bridging the digital divide. However, educators must become keenly aware of their skill limitations and technical capacity prior to committing GIS products and services to community partners.

While CM projects are equally effective in alternative learning programs as they are in public and private schools, it is important to recognize that each entity is driven by different goals, standards, and educational objectives. In schools and programs that have adopted place-based, community-based, project-based, inquiry-based, or education for sustainability teaching models, the introduction of a Community Mapping

"Rarely is a map created to tell us the way people feel about a place. Our sense of place is in fact very much a product of perceptions—individual, societal, and cultural. And a map is more often than not a tacit cultural covenant that in turn affects our perception of a place." —Christopher Castle, *EcoPsychology*

Community Mapping projects connect people to one another . . . through investigations that create greater understanding. . . .

**CONNECTIONS AND CONTINUITY
GUIDING PRINCIPLE**

project will be easiest because schedules and administrative support already provide for hands-on and real-world learning opportunities. Where these types of approaches have not yet been adopted, your team must work harder to keep the project scope small and to build the essential community–school bridges. In all cases, it is paramount to keep school administrators and group leaders advised of and even involved in the various phases of project development and deployment and to demonstrate how your students are meeting academic standards and goals throughout the process. The life skills and workplace experience that the youth gain as a result of

working with community mentors are also important benefits to highlight in the documentation of any CM project.

Clearly defining the academic standards and goals that will be met by the CM project is a vital step that sets the framework for keeping students on track and assessing their work. Community partners who understand the academic goals involved will be better able to support them as they guide student activities and work with educators to ensure quality in performance and products. Partners who do not understand the goals may not fully appreciate the amount of time and energy it may take to complete various skills development

exercises in preparation for the actual work. As mentioned, school administrators will also be more likely to support the projects when they see the standards-based approach your team has adopted.

Documentation may take the form of listing academic standards that will be met and constructing rubrics for assessing student work. Many CM project teams adopt more of a client–contractor approach, in which students (the contractors) continue to refine their products until the community partner (the client) is satisfied. Otherwise, students would be able to turn in "C" work and be done with their assignment, leaving the partner's expectations quite unfulfilled and their interest in future projects quite diminished.

Teamwork

One area of project design that is easily and preferably tackled by students is identifying tasks and constructing teams around them. Depending on class size, it may make sense for all students to be involved in each of the identified tasks, for example: research, data collection, GIS applications, and oral presentations. With large classes or more complex projects, the students may desire to work on specific tasks they are most interested in, such as conducting public surveys, doing historical research, or writing press releases as part of a publicity campaign. Each team must lead and organize its own charge and also coordinate with the other teams to make sure that the final product is coherent and complete.

Equally important is their commitment to stay in contact with their community mentor, who can keep them heading in the right direction.

Encouraging students to take responsibility for shaping their teams and then working together to accomplish a common mission can result in the following extraordinary life lessons:

- emergence of leaders and development of leadership skills
- pressure on nonperformers to come through for the team
- confidence building from a job well done
- introspective insights and revelations about themselves and their teammates
- learning to deal with stress over responsibilities
- motivation to try new skills on behalf of the team
- problem-solving and troubleshooting skills development
- communication skills development (writing and speaking)
- experiencing success

"It is necessary to understand what GIS is, how it operates, its strengths and weaknesses, and the many concepts that make it useful to various applications."

BRUCE DAVIS
GIS: A VISUAL APPROACH

The mapping component

By the time your project team starts to earnestly plan what to map and how, you have already determined whether you will be using GIS software and computers for data analysis and map generation and possibly GPS units for data collection. In coming to this decision, you considered the following criteria:

- Appropriateness of GIS technology:
  - *Would a hand-drawn map suffice?*
- Are you adding to an existing GIS project or creating a new one?
- Availability of computers, GIS software and suitable GPS units:
  - *Do partner and school computers have compatible platforms?*
  - *Do GPS units store data points for direct downloading into computers?*
  - *Do you have the correct software and protocol for transferring GPS data into GIS?*
- Prerequisite computer skills of the partner, educators, and students
- Prior GIS training and experience of project team members

- Availability of a GIS specialist to prepare project base maps, if needed:
  - *GIS professional consultant*
  - *City or county GIS staff member*
  - *Trained school technology coordinator*
  - *Community partner provides a GIS specialist*
- Readiness of educators to train students in necessary GIS/GPS skills and applications
- Availability of a GIS specialist to support student GIS/GPS training and project development
- Commitment of partner and GIS specialist to provide quality control support

You have also consulted local agencies, GIS professionals, and other community specialists to learn what kinds of pertinent data are available, their degree of compatibility, and the amount of work required to collect, assimilate, and analyze the data. Different agencies collect data using different projections, such as UTM or state plane, and this can cause compatibility problems if you hope to combine aerial photos from one agency and geographic features—such as roads and rivers—from another. Finally, as previously emphasized, *you must fit all the steps into your available time. Do you have sufficient time to devote to each step? Do you know how long each step will realistically take? Have you allowed time for unexpected hurdles?*

Pulling it all together

You have gathered information, collected ideas, recruited available resources, drafted a project and curriculum plan, and weighed the pros and cons of proceeding with a fairly well-defined scope of work for your CM project. This conceptualization and planning process may not have advanced in a linear or straightforward manner, but rather with multiple concerns being investigated simultaneously by different participants or subgroups. However your project plan actually comes together, you must keep the big picture in sight as you deal with the minutiae. The following summary provides a benchmark for judging how well your initial project plan measures against the big picture.

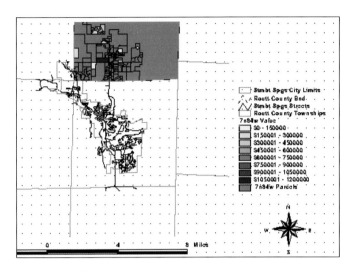

The possibility of packing lots of data into colorful maps makes GIS an attractive tool. But is it appropriate for the needs of your project?

CM project conceptualization planner

Purpose: To develop the project idea by describing it and considering where it fits into the big picture from each partner's perspective.

- Why are you doing this project?
  Describe the benefits, tangible and intangible, to all team members. As your project team discusses why you are doing this project, you are developing a shared vision that describes the benefits to all partners. This piece also has future value for public relations and for selling the project idea to others.

- How does your project advance the partner's work in the community?

- How does your project advance the academic goals and standards of the school or class?

- Describe your project simply and clearly as if you had to summarize it for a newspaper reporter.
  By writing and agreeing on a summary of the project, community partners and educators will discover whether they have a mutual understanding of the project. They can also use this paragraph later in presentations and press releases.

- Will the project be an add-on, replace parts of an existing curriculum, or be carried out as an independent study course or extracurricular project?
  Because Community Mapping projects offer unique and exciting opportunities for learning, teachers may undertake a project without fully considering the effect it will have on their curriculum. It is worth spending time considering whether the project will be an add-on, will replace parts of the existing curriculum or be carried out as an independent study course or an extracurricular project. If it is an add-on, will there be adequate time to do a thorough job on the project or will either the regular curriculum or the project suffer? If it replaces part of the existing curriculum, what does it replace?

CM projects are intended to be replacement curricula or lessons, not add-ons. Some educators, however, may be more comfortable introducing their initial CM project as an after-school activity before integrating it fully into their curriculum—and this is okay!

- Community partners should also consider potential impacts on their work and on deadlines.
  Involving schools and students may add time to a project and take more staff participation than conducting the work in-house. Community partners and project mentors will need to plan for this and be able to justify the effort to the rest of their organization or office.

- What does success look like?
  To the community partner, to the educators, and to the students.

Implementation and administration

If the implementation phase of a Community Mapping project had to be characterized by one key word, it would be communication. Ongoing communication—and lots of it, at all levels—is paramount to successfully carrying out a CM project. Especially if you are trying out a single CM project on your own without access to CMP support and facilitation, these communication channels must be consciously kept open throughout the project. Many CM project teams have judiciously elected to have the students stay directly in touch with their community mentors, knowing that reminders about expectation levels would likely be necessary. These types of student–mentor relationships may be new to everyone, so be prepared to spend a little class time reviewing the communication plan, ideally with the project mentor and other community experts present.

Working with community members
The earlier determination of who would fill the primary project mentor role for a CM project was based on individual suitability, availability, needs, and interest. Multiple subject matter experts may participate in CM projects at various times, but generally only one primary project mentor maintains consistency of direction and leadership. More complex mentor models can be incorporated into a CM project, but only one community organization and individual within that

organization should serve as the primary project mentor.

Undoubtedly the most rewarding project experience that students speak of is the opportunity to work directly with community members, particularly the primary project mentor. On the other hand, the most challenging aspect of CM project work for students is working with community members in general. What does this apparent paradox mean to CM project teams and the relationships that must drive the mutual mission forward? How do students effectively deal with these real-world challenges?

We have found that regular communication concerning each community member's availability—including when (dates) and for how long (hours)—is paramount to helping students know when they should or could schedule contacts and meetings. Time is a decisive resource that may change as the project advances. Building community members' availability into the master timeline for the project should be an early order of business, but monitoring their availability and making necessary scheduling adjustments as the project advances should also occur on a regular basis. A sudden business trip may preclude a community specialist's ability to make good on a planned commitment unless the project schedule can be modified accordingly or a substitute specialist provided. Project events and deadlines for interim products are best scheduled around periods when the mentor can provide adequate prior support to the students and educators can dedicate sufficient class time to accomplish the necessary preparation and skills development. Similarly, students need to respect project timelines and mentor availability and communicate their own potential scheduling problems in advance of a conflict. Students will gain valuable experience in time management as a result.

Working with mentors: How to help them help you

1 Before calling, you should have an idea of what you need from the mentor written down.
Develop these ideas through discussions with your groups, teachers, and other adults.

2 Mentors usually have full-time jobs, so they need advance notice of meetings and field trips . . .
but if something comes up, call them! They may be able to meet with you on short notice. If you have an urgent need to meet with a mentor, you can always apologize for the short notice and ask when is the earliest convenient time they could meet with you.

3 The person you contact may not be the right expert, so ask them if they can help you with certain tasks.
If not, who else might be able to help you? If your search dries up, contact one of the back-up contacts listed below for alternate ideas or to help you identify interim specialists (if someone is temporarily unavailable).

Back-up Contacts

A Name: Phone:
  E-mail: Alternate Phone:
  Contact Notes:

B Name: Phone:
  E-mail: Alternate Phone:
  Contact Notes:

4 Mentors need to know what you expect them to do, but you should also ask them what you need to know or do before they help you tackle your task.
Be prepared to tell the mentor what your level of understanding is about the topic. Make a list of "to-dos" for you and your mentor before ending the discussion and confirm that you both have a copy. If, for example, you ask a mentor to help you locate fences on your

project site using a GPS unit, the mentor would want to schedule time for classroom instruction, data collection planning, and GPS practice before meeting you at the project site to locate fences. They may also want you to be trained by another specialist and call them back when you know some basics about what you need to do. Ask mentors to describe what they are willing to help you do—they may not be willing to cover everything you need help with.

5 **Some mentors may need reminders.**
It is good practice to call them the day before a meeting, especially if your plans were made a few days or weeks in advance. If you are expecting your mentor to deliver or do something by a certain date, it is also good practice to call them in advance of that date to confirm that they are on schedule with what they promised. Remember to thank them for honoring their commitment.

6 **Follow-up confirmations are always worth your time.**
It is a good practice to call your mentor to confirm that they received the items that you sent to them or to let them know that you received their delivery to you. Neither the mail system nor technology are as dependable as we would like them to be. E-mails, faxes, postal carriers, and answering machines can be unreliable modes of communication and exchange, so it is good practice to call the mentor directly to confirm that you did or did not receive their delivery as expected. Also call them to confirm that they received important material you sent to them.

7 **Mentors like to feel useful and that their time is well spent, so respect their time and their desire for efficient meetings.**
Try to give them the full picture of your project so they can help you streamline activities or schedule them efficiently. Ask them how you can help arrange for an effective and efficient meeting.

8 **Mentors like appreciation, so let them know you appreciate their time and commitment to your project.**
Thank-you notes, e-mails, public commendations and awards, and other gestures of appreciation would also be well received and go a long way toward cementing their commitment to helping you succeed.

9 **When frustrated, challenged, or needing to "vent," first think of who may help you most.**
It may be your teacher, project team, back-up contact, mentor, or family members. Ask yourself and others who might be able to help you. Building effective working relationships requires working through problems sensibly. Try to understand the mentor's point of view and always avoid burning bridges!

Depending on the age and maturity of the students, educators may want to give them the responsibility for initiating communications with their project mentor and other community experts to the degree possible, providing timely guidance and support as necessary. The less educators do for their students, the more students will gain from their experience. The previous tip sheet was developed for students getting ready to work directly with community mentors and experts for the first time. These may be helpful guidelines for your new project team to consider.

Effective and coordinated communication is a paramount concern when many people and different groups collaborate on a complex project.

TELEPHONE ETIQUETTE

It is important to follow basic etiquette rules when using the telephone for business or formal purposes.

Timing
- Always call at least ten days to two weeks before you wish to meet with someone
- Do not wait until the last moment! Leave enough time before the proposed meeting or due date so that you may call the person again if you are not successful with your first contact

When speaking to someone
- State your name and purpose for the call
- Give specific times, dates, places, or material you are requesting
- Write it down!
- Repeat the key times, dates, places, and material to the person before hanging up
- Thank them!

When leaving a phone message
- State your name, date, and time of call
- Give a specific purpose for your call
- Leave a date, time, and return number at which you may be reached
- Use a time planner to set and record a date and time to call the person in case your call is not returned
- Thank them!

If you are asking for someone's time or expertise, communication is your responsibility.

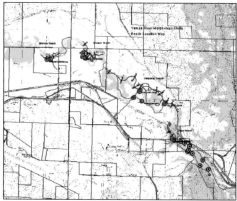

Communication must get off on the right foot at the beginning of the project implementation phase, as this is often the point at which students are first brought into the process and the commitments are cast in clay. Following is a summary of typical agreements educators and the community partner (or project mentor) will have made during the previous conceptualization and planning phase that should be reviewed and further developed with the students when they are first introduced to the CM project.

Making a team commitment

- Educator, students, primary project mentor, and other community specialists accept responsibilities and timelines and agree to proceed.

- The commitment may be formal or informal, but should be based on a written outline, proposal, rubrics, or scope-of-work document. Students may become directly involved in developing portions of this working agreement. Educators should include the basic academic standards and educational goals the students must meet.

- Identify the need for additional specialists and technical experts early and factor in an orientation event and information package as appropriate. Students can help the team consider the range of support that might be required, from GIS experts and community planners to botanists and historians.

- Reach a consensus on the quality of acceptable work. Is "C" work acceptable? What constitutes "A" work? If students turn in "C" work, can the project mentor return it for qualitative improvements until it is right?

- Factor formative assessments into the timeline. Educators and community partners should all provide students with regular, substantive feedback. Grading student performance against rubrics or other criteria is strongly recommended as one method of providing both timely feedback and the incentive to achieve. The project mentor, in particular, should agree to review students' draft products and provide timely, substantive feedback.

- Reach an agreement on the quantity of work required. Have students prioritize tasks and then agree to accomplish a minimum number of tasks. Once these requisite tasks are completed to the satisfaction of the entire team, the team may agree to complete additional tasks as a bonus to the community partner and extra credit for the students.

- Determine deadlines for relevant, interim products and stick to the deadlines to the degree possible. Educators and the project mentor agree in advance to monitor progress against the master timeline regularly and make adjustments to the schedule and project scope as warranted.

"If students had something interesting so that they could see a point to what they were learning, I think there would be a lot more interest and a lot higher grades, a lot higher enthusiasm in school."

YAMPA VALLEY STUDENT

Community Mapping projects and
place-based learning

Place-based education is the foundation of the CMP model. Each community's unique blend of history, culture, traditions, and physical features provides a living laboratory for today's youth to investigate how the different parts actually relate to one another and shape a whole system. The community provides a dynamic, boundless, complex system that students can study, scrutinize, and ultimately enrich with their own understanding. Why are more and more schools and alternative learning programs adopting *experiential pedagogy*—both inside and outside their communities—over long-established teaching doctrines? Perhaps the relevant context more effectively expands students' awareness of the contributions each of the disciplines make, both individually and collectively, to the character and operation of a community—and ultimately the world. Biologists must often apply statistics and deductive reasoning skills to manage our living resources, just as chefs may need to apply math and marketing skills to create enticing menus that insure a constant stream of patrons. The process of learning may still be hard via a place-based approach, but it will be pertinent and rewarding. Place-based investigations can be made even more enlightening and poignant by integrating a dynamic mapping component—and most

Sense of place is personal and local in nature, and its expression can be as simply rendered as this hand-drawn map.

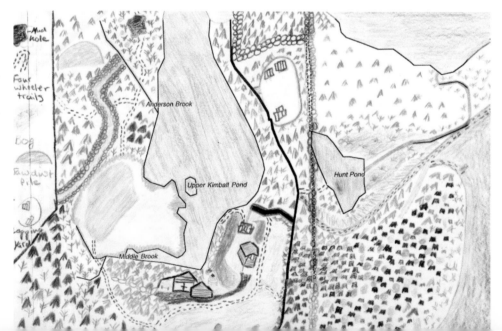

every investigation of the real world harbors at least one "mappable" aspect.

An integral part of place-based education is the process of inquiry and discovery in developing a connection to the local community and environment, while meeting curriculum objectives and academic standards. By the time the CM project is scheduled to begin, your curriculum framework should be sketched out as a result of previous collaborative conceptualization and planning work. You have left considerable room and flexibility in the project design and curriculum to accommodate student interests and ideas. As one Rural Challenge Research Associate observed of place-based projects, "When students select the topic, idea, or issue, it tends to be fuller, aided by a large personal dimension." CM projects are designed to give students range, but also to give them guidance.

The CMP model provides that educators know how to effectively develop curricula within their own disciplines. Some educators, however, may not have had prior experience leading community-based projects, developing place-based lesson plans or introducing a new technology. With an understanding of the basic principles, place-based activities are easiest to adopt, as these can often emulate an innovative variation of the traditional field trip. Community-based, collaborative projects can pose minimal challenges if healthy communications and project management practices are maintained, as mentioned earlier and covered in more depth in CM training. Introducing GIS technologies to students, however,

requires that the project's scope and complexity reflect the technical capacity and confidence of the responsible educators, as well as the students' technical aptitude. Technical demands that exceed an educator's comfort level may lead to frustration and confusion among students, as well as the potential for a failed project. On the other hand, some students with no prior GIS exposure, but who have exceptional technical capabilities and proclivity, have been known to take over a project's GIS tasks and move well beyond their instructor's skill level.

Introducing Community Mapping projects and GIS technologies

GIS and mapping skills are best viewed as tools for achieving both academic and community goals—not as the focus of activity-driven curricula. Certainly the introduction to GIS and the CM project may involve initial exercises and practice activities, but these should quickly lead to project-related tasks. The CMP model references this type of introduction as the vertical slice approach.

The vertical slice approach involves limiting the introduction of a new technology or topic to those aspects that apply to the immediate task or project, including only pertinent background, context, and foundation-setting lessons. In order to engage students as soon as possible in the real work of their project—which is where they are most motivated—curricula should streamline the project introductory phase to enable more hands-on, directly relevant tasks and experiences. How much GIS do students really need to know to carry out a CM project? What can you do in advance to allow your students to experiment with and experience GIS without having to first build it from scratch?

Depending on the grade level involved, prior GIS training, and whether GIS software will actually be used, most instructors will want to introduce a CM project, including mapping concepts and GIS generally, as outlined below, with emphasis on the disciplines they are teaching. Of course, a few prerequisites for integrating GIS applications include access to a computer lab with GIS software and proven computer skills, such as file management and working with word documents, spreadsheets, and the Internet.

Vertical slice approach

Teaching selected capabilities and mechanics— enough to effectively apply the technology to an immediate task. It does not entail dedicated instruction on the full scope of technical skills and applications. If five different methods lead to the same end point, teach one method and reinforce it immediately through hands-on practice and application.

Introducing a Community Mapping project

1 **Overview of CM project purpose and goals with the community mentor**
If possible, introduce other community experts, GIS specialists, local planners, local leaders, and skilled "-ologists" and professionals as appropriate, ideally including a site visit and discussion of project goals and partner roles.

2 **Review educational objectives, knowledge, and other skills to be learned by students with both the students and community mentor**

3 **Agree upon project objectives, timelines, and products (quality and quantity), and adopt this as a contract of work**
What does success look like?

4 **Optional mapping concepts and exercises**
   (a) What are maps?
   (b) What kinds of maps are there?
   (c) How do landmarks and events relate to each other and the landscape, such as spatial relationships (adjacency, connectivity, containment, unions, and so on)?
   (d) How do different map projections affect viewers' perception of the information?
   (e) Find, download from the Internet, or draw different types of maps
   (f) Trace different features from the same map—for example forest boundary, roads, lakes and rivers, city boundaries, and so on—onto overhead transparencies and project them in various combinations to demonstrate GIS layering
   (g) Other topics as applicable: contouring, scale, coordinate systems

5 What is GIS?

   (a) Overview: Demonstrate a GIS project at the outset to create a visual context of GIS capabilities.

Include a few features beyond the immediate needs of the CM project to stimulate student interest in the potential of GIS to enhance understanding and decision making through data management and analysis and graphic presentation (i.e., hotlinks, buffers, charts, 3–D, queries, legend editing, editing tables, and so forth).

Note: Especially when CM projects may only focus on one aspect of a larger issue, the students need to see where the project is ultimately headed and how their piece fits into the big picture. If possible, allow time for students to actually experiment with a GIS project on their own computers.

   (b) Review types and sources of various data: point, line, polygon, images, text, data attributes, and so on.

Sources: CM workshop toolkits, city and county planners, Internet; ArcLessons (ArcView curricula on the ESRI Web site: www.arclessons.com).

   (c) Review relational data tables (databases) in preparation for managing data in a GIS.

   (d) Review how a GIS can be applied to real-world problem solving and decision making. How would it apply to the current CM project?

   (e) Review the specific data requirements and products of the CM project among the students, mentor, and educators. Do we need photos and descriptive text? Who has existing data we can use? How will the new data be collected? Where will the base map come from?

Note: Having a project base map ready for the students to start building on immediately is highly recommended.

   (f) Present basics of how GPS technology works, incorporating applicable math principles Practice GPS data collection skills in the field, even outside the school building, as soon as possible.

   (g) Review and practice data collection standards and protocol, data accuracy, and data attributes of the CM project with guidance from educators and community mentor.

   (h) Explore what types of data you might not want to collect or map for public use, since "if you map it, they might come." Consider sacred archaeological sites, endangered species habitat, historic landmarks on private lands, dangerous sites, and so forth.

6 Students help define specific tasks and guide the formation of task teams.

7 Begin GIS skills training and project work in a systematic manner with frequent communication, data collection field trips, and assessments factored into the timeline.

   (a) Practice GPS data collection again; learn how to add GPS data to a GIS.

   (b) Plan data collection strategies and field trips to the project site(s); execute strategies.

   (c) Learn GIS basics using packaged exercises at first and actual project data soon after:
     –Working with spatial data, querying data, managing tabular data, analyzing spatial relationships, presenting information, creating your own data.

   (d) Apply GIS skills to manage and analyze data and create interim products.

   (e) Move toward final products and presentation of information.

"We have very limited resources and this type of project helps us. We are always getting into problems when hard data is needed and we don't have it. This is hard data."

ON THE NUISANCE BEAR SIGHTINGS COMMUNITY MAPPING PROJECT CARRIED OUT BY
A SINGLE MIDDLE SCHOOL STUDENT, HIS TEACHER, AND A COMMUNITY MENTOR

Eighty students helped a Division of Wildlife mentor collect data characterizing a new wildlife area, and prepared a comprehensive management plan with the aid of GIS.

The basic outline on the previous pages is intended to reinforce the value of allowing enough time in the beginning to fully review the intent of both the project and the application of maps and GIS with the students. The methodology and manner of introducing technical tools and concepts to students is as important as matching the degree of difficulty with their capacity to learn. For example, the introductory phase would ideally begin with the mentor leading a fun site visit, with creative, relevant, thought-provoking group discussions while in the field. *Why would tracking and mapping large game and livestock road kill on a specific stretch of highway be of interest to wildlife managers and the*

community? What maps and analyses could we do to shed light on this problem? How could this information be used to help us better manage the resources and also keep our highways safe for travelers? Accordingly, CM workshops train educators to effectively teach GIS to students within the context of a real-world project, using proven tools, activities, and a replicable approach that follows the general outline above. It goes further in providing educators with a foundation of project design, management, and assessment strategies that can effectively raise the quality and efficacy of their team's project planning and implementation efforts.

Creating a sense of ownership

An essential goal in building the framework for a rewarding and dynamic CM project experience that fully engages students and establishes realistic expectations is to incite a sense of ownership in the project. As mentioned earlier, the planning and conceptualization phase offers ideal opportunities for students to become directly involved in proposing and developing a CM project idea from the very beginning, if schedules permit and educators are amenable. When individuals' ideas are recognized, they will

generally want to see their proposals materialize and will help make that happen.

One method for establishing ownership during the implementation phase is to encourage students to become actively involved in identifying problems inherent in their CM project that they could investigate and help to resolve. Why is the project important to others? How will the results enlighten others and help them appreciate their community and care for its resources? This approach is based on a marketing technique for generating buy-in, which is to "sell a problem, not a solution." Educators and community mentors would be wise to lead the students toward identifying the issues that need to be studied.

CM projects often require students to interact with the public to collect information concerning the issue they are studying. This situation can offer yet another means of creating ownership in the project by allowing students to take the initiative to design, publicize, and co-lead (with their project mentor) facilitated meetings, informational meetings, or dedicated surveys. Empowering students to represent their class, let alone their project, can impart a sense of responsibility to be prepared and to do their best.

Another way to foster ownership is to have students who are already familiar with GIS help demonstrate its capabilities or assist fellow students, acting much like a teaching assistant. Several CM project teams in Colorado lend experienced GIS students to lower grade levels—both the younger students and upper classmen like this arrangement and it certainly contributes to student learning on all sides. The upper classmen develop confidence, critical thinking skills, leadership skills, and professional ethics as a bonus to their academic achievement. The challenge is to guide students toward a vision without providing step-by-step, cookbook instructions.

Getting to final products

We started this section by discussing communication and we will end it by reinforcing communication as a fundamental key to success. This time the emphasis is on conducting substantive, formative assessments of student work throughout the CM project—a way of giving students regular, constructive feedback on how they are doing. These assessments also provide opportunities for students to give their teachers and mentor timely clues about how the

Teachers being taught: the foremost task for teachers in a CM project is to instill a sense of ownership in their students.

process is working (or not working) and the quality of support they are receiving (or not receiving).

Following are a few basic ways that student progress, achievement, and even nonperformance can be acknowledged and their work redirected as necessary. Even CM projects conducted as independent studies or extracurricular activities deserve ongoing critiques so that the students, educators, and community mentor have a good sense that student efforts and actions will indeed lead to the desired outcomes and that the experience is as rewarding as possible for everyone involved. Regular infusions of approval and guidance can certainly make the experience rewarding for all participants.

Guidance in the field and feedback in the classroom are critical to student progress.

Providing student feedback and direction through formative assessments

- Before the project begins, administer standard pretests to determine the base knowledge of students in the key areas of technical and academic learning they are expected to master; at the end of the project compare pretest results to posttest results to determine the degree to which the CM project affected student learning; standard pre- and posttests applicable to CM projects are available from The Orton Family Foundation.

- Grade individuals on the quality of interim products against project rubrics, contract, or specific assignments.

- Grade task teams on the quality of interim products, encouraging and rewarding teamwork.

- For projects that are divided up into task teams, look for evidence of inter-task team communication and coordination; have students determine how team interactions can be improved to positively effect the integrity of the final product.

- Require task team representatives to give oral updates to the entire project team.
  – Rotate speakers; grade or mark as completed; give feedback on ways to improve speaking skills.

- Test or quiz students on technical skills and curricular material covered.

- Provide opportunities for extra credit.
  - Teach other students a new skill such as the use of GPS units for data collection, or how to measure pH, or researching a specific topic related to the project and curriculum objectives.

- Review interim products and provide feedback to all students in a group setting; discuss general problems and encourage students to offer or negotiate resolutions.

- Post the project's master timeline on the wall for the purpose of tracking the progress of the entire class; use the chart to also display timely reminders, thought-provoking questions, and task-specific kudos that encourage movement toward project completion.

- Lead full project team discussions on topics such as:
  - *What does success look like?*
  - *Where are we on the road to success?*
  - *What do we each need to do to get to success?*
  - *What do you understand about your mapping project?*
  - *What don't you understand?*

- Develop progress report formats that can be administered by the educators and turned over to the mentor for review, with consequences for missing deadlines.

Dissemination and information sharing

Maps shape our perception of place
The information that maps contain is as important as the process used to arrive at the final product. Maps must be talked about and shared to provoke thoughts and feelings of place. They must be studied and questioned to promote understanding.

Map products generated by students in collaboration with their project mentor will take many forms, so the best way to disseminate them will vary between projects. Whether the end product is intended to reside on an agency computer, a public Web site or town hall wall, the young creators certainly need to learn to communicate their findings to their partner and the public in a coherent, relevant way. This is the ultimate test of how well the students understood their mission and how successful they were in meeting the expectations of their teachers and mentors.

Public interactions and project publicity
CM projects may require that students work closely with the public throughout their investigation. This presents educators with a golden opportunity to shift the responsibility for organizing public interactions to their students. Whether it involves conducting interviews or public surveys, facilitating meetings, or reporting out project goals and interim findings to the community, students can learn valuable life lessons from arranging these events, including related publicity, themselves. Of course, it is necessary to match initiatives like this with the age and capabilities of the students—the younger grades may only be capable of planning and carrying out a short presentation, for example, and not actually organizing or leading key events.

One group of high school students in Colorado formed a special task team around the publicity needs of their project and recruited a local journalist to mentor them. They had to communicate and coordinate with the other project task teams to correctly reflect the message their entire project team needed them to deliver. The guidelines below resulted from the publicity task team's journey into the kingdom of public relations. Their experiences in dealing with the public may help make the road smoother for other CM project teams faced with a similar challenge.

Because CM projects deal with current events, there is a continuing need for public display and forums that may elicit direction from new sources.

PUBLICITY STRATEGY FOR PUBLIC EVENTS

Compiled for the Yampa Valley Community Mapping Program with help from the *Steamboat Today/Pilot*

1 Research other events that may be planned for the same time as early as possible.
    • Call the city council, the county commissioners' office, school district office, and so forth, to ask about other events planned for the same time and let them know what you are planning.
    • Six to eight weeks in advance is not too early.
    • Be sure the location you need is available—reserve space as soon as possible.

2 Let others know the date and general purpose as soon as possible.
    "It is never too early to let us know about these events," says Jennifer Bartlett, reporter/mentor.

3 Who should be informed? (at least a month in advance, and sooner if possible)
    • Local Arts and Education reporter.
    • City council.
    • County commissioners.
    • Interested organizations and community groups.

4 Do the research for a press release as early as possible, preferably five or six weeks or more in advance of the event.
    • Ask others (such as teachers and mentors) why the event is important—collect quotes!
    • Verify that the information you gather is correct. Who can help you verify the information?
    • Develop an outline of up to five major points you want to make in a press release (such as when and where the event will occur, why it is important to attend, what students will do at event).

5 At least four weeks prior to your event, contact your reporter to coordinate the press release. Reporters would appreciate even more notice if possible! Remember, you will need to work around their schedule and deadlines. They are excited to work directly with students throughout all phases of developing and implementing your publicity plan—*if* you notify them well in advance of your event.

Other Publicity Avenues
    • Record your own public service announcement (PSA) with a local radio station. Contact them as soon as possible to arrange the taping.
    • Draft a PSA to fax to radio stations. If you cannot arrange to record your own PSA, have the stations read your press release. Radio PSA's will necessarily need to be short and to the point!
    • Make flyers to distribute and post in strategic locations around the community. Think about your target audience—where do they go? Who else can help spread the word? Here are some suggestions: local nonprofits, relevant retail stores, school bulletin boards and newsletters, direct mailing to community leaders and parents.

Other guidelines
    • Follow up on all communications. If you send a fax or e-mail, call the recipient to make sure they received it.
    • Confirm appointments in advance. If you have set a meeting time, call one or two days prior to the meeting to confirm.
    • Confirm commitments. If someone has promised to deliver information or materials to you, call them prior to the delivery time to confirm that they will be able to come through as expected.

PRESS RELEASE   **PRESS RELEASE**

To: Steamboat Today/Pilot
Date: December 8, 1999
Contact: (Student Name)
           Steamboat Springs High School 2003 FLITE Class
           970/xxx-xxxx

Students To Host Open House for the Steamboat Springs Wildlife Area Management Plan

Steamboat Springs High School freshmen and the Colorado Division of Wildlife (CDOW) will host an Open House at 7 P.M. on December 15th, to share information about the Steamboat Springs Wildlife Area Management Plan the students are developing with CDOW.

Please come to show your support and to share your ideas on wildlife and wildlife-related recreation management issues for this newly acquired state wildlife area, located south of Steamboat Springs near Highway 131 and CR 14F. This project represents a joint effort between the CDOW, Steamboat Springs High School freshmen, Lowell Whiteman High School students, Yampa Valley Community Mapping Project, The Orton Family Foundation, Yampa Valley Legacy Education Initiative, and many community members working with the students.

Join us for an evening of learning, sharing ideas, and recognition of our talented and hard-working students at the Steamboat Springs High School commons area on Wednesday, December 15th, from 7:00–8:30 P.M.

For more information, please contact Steamboat Springs High School at xxx-xxxx or Libbie Miller at the CDOW.

Above is an example of an early press release developed by a student working with a journalist–mentor. It promotes a public meeting designed to give an overview of the project to the community and then solicit public feedback on specific resource management issues the students were tackling with their project mentor. It was distributed to the local radio station and newspaper. The students also developed a flyer that they reproduced and posted at strategic places around the community to further publicize the event. The publicity task team enlisted the help of their classmates to brainstorm central locations, ranging from the local grocery and retail stores to city and county offices, and then distributed the flyers accordingly. After the event the community partner reported that more people (over one hundred) showed up for this meeting than previous ones (drawing less than twenty attendees), largely because many parents were drawn to support their children. Hence, civic involvement is either contagious or a direct result of good parenting plus being around kids energized by their own contributions to the community.

The CMP model strongly recommends sharing information beyond the walls of your CM project to the extent possible. For example, keep the media

> *"Public display and forums enhance the value of projects, build student confidence, promote civic participation, and foster stronger community–school relationships."*
>
> **SHARING RESULTS**
> **GUIDING PRINCIPLE**

aware of project meetings, workshops, field trips, and presentations as a matter of habit. Especially when projects may not explicitly require community involvement, adult project team members should make a concerted effort to keep local reporters informed of opportunities to cover CM project activities and developments throughout the project. Reporters love to catch students working with their community mentor, both in the classroom and in the field, as well as demonstrating their newly acquired GIS skills to others. Many project teams elect to present their projects to city and county officials—reporters will often jump to cover these events since student citizenry is a noteworthy concept. Maintaining community awareness of students' new role in shaping local perspectives is definitely worth cultivating as this one commitment can fuel students' motivation levels considerably.

Final project presentations
The Community Mapping Program recognizes the value of having educators, community partners, and especially students share their project experiences and results with each other and with the public. One or more opportunities should be provided during the school year for students to practice their oral communication skills in preparation for a final public presentation. This will force them to organize their work and be prepared to address questions from the audience, such as: *What were your overall objectives? What did you produce? How did you produce it? What challenges did you overcome? What did you learn? How did the project tie into your course work? How will the community partner use their new mapping products? If you could do this project over, what would you do differently?*

The extraordinary benefits that come from sharing results beyond projects have, in fact, made this practice a guiding principle in the CMP model. While this principle can be met in a variety of ways, the bottom line is to require that students present at least their final results to the public or to other groups outside their immediate project team. If your project team cannot find another planned event to tag onto, you might consider setting up student presentations for county commissioners and community leaders during one of their regular sessions.

Another excellent option is to assemble a mixed audience near the end of the school year or at the completion of the CM project dedicated solely to CM projects and student presentations. These dedicated events should be widely publicized using all available media and local reporters should be notified well in advance so they are available to cover the event. Invitees might include other students, teachers, and administrators from the school district, parents, community members, and an assortment of community leaders. Sending personal invitations to community leaders and individuals outside the school system is more effective than relying entirely on a mass media campaign.

Allowing time for questions to the students and engaging discussions among project team members and the audience is highly recommended. The interactions are not only good for the students—they

How can we use GIS and other visual tools to promote cooperative education, planning, and problem-solving partnerships between communities and schools?

must be ready to take the spotlight and deliver—but they can also lead to greater community and school support of and participation in CM projects.

A wonderful, though unforeseen, observation we made in the process of lining up student speakers for presentations was that many actually sought out these opportunities to represent their work, team, and school. Another surprise was that students with a history of poor or troubled academic performance found these speaking engagements satisfying and exciting, impressing their peers and audiences with remarkable presentations. Being observed achieving success, especially by peers, has tremendous confidence-building potential. Educators and the community mentor need to help students adequately prepare for these public presentations to minimize their risk for failure—in fact, striving to eliminate the risk entirely should be the ultimate goal.

Of course, at every information-sharing gathering and project presentation event, opportunities should be made for acknowledging the work of all team members—students, educators, and community partners—and for recognizing the special contributions of selected individuals who truly deserve to be singled out as role models, leaders, troubleshooters, or risk-takers. Our experience has also impelled us to save time for students to express their gratitude to mentors, fellow students, teachers, and community specialists for their support; they will frequently offer words of appreciation if given the opportunity.

Using the Internet for sharing information
The Orton Family Foundation offers a central location for sharing CM project plans, assessment tools, student products, and other project-related materials through its Web site, *www.communitymap.org*. Ideally, students who have a penchant for Web page development would lead the task as a requirement of the project and receive appropriate credit for successfully posting their work (or at least submitting it to The Orton Family Foundation).

Participating schools and partnering organizations are similarly encouraged to post representative products on their own Web sites and provide direct links to the CM Web site referenced above. The commitment to share results not only gives other project teams access to a valuable and growing knowledge base, but also validates the students' work and contributions to their community.

A thorough set of guidelines, or template, for determining which materials to assemble into a well-organized case study, is found on the following pages. A secondary benefit of using this template from the outset of a CM project is that it can provide timely clues about additional

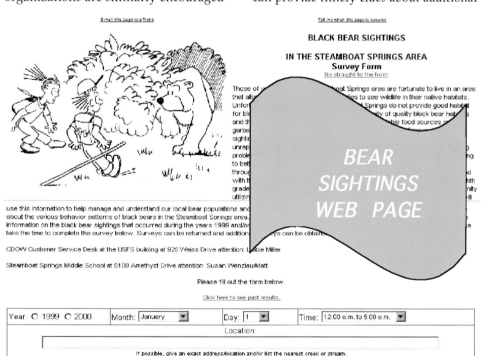

The Internet and World Wide Web have revolutionized the means students have for sharing their work.

"GIS is a toolbox for exploring the world."

RICHARD AUDET AND GAIL LUDWIG
GIS IN SCHOOLS (2000)

materials and activities that, if developed and incorporated into the project, may facilitate progress in the right direction. An excellent method of compiling pertinent documentation is to use an electronic project portfolio to file materials digitally, including photographs of work in progress and interim products, as they are generated by any of the team members. This method offers a way to standardize formats and nomenclature for ready application in a Web format. With an entire classroom of students generating images, maps, text, data, and research pieces and educators and community partners developing instruments of project management, instruction, and assessment, it is easy to imagine the volume of valuable documentation a CM project can produce. Why should others have to create from scratch what is already here for the sharing? Further, if certain materials or methods did not work well, why would you want to find this out the hard way?

Because information is only as good as its accessibility, all CM project teams are strongly encouraged to make their experiences available—both the success stories and the lessons learned—via The Orton Family Foundation's Community Mapping Program Web site. Representative project materials and case studies would either be posted on the Foundation's site or a direct link provided to your site to give widespread access to our growing base of CM experiences and wisdom and to give your team credit for making community mapping possibilities happen!

Template for Community Mapping project case studies

Compiled by Margaret Berglund, Graduate Student Intern, Yampa Valley Community Mapping Program, August 20, 2001. [Revised May 12, 2002]

Project title:

Partnered organizations:

Partnered schools:

Project duration (dates and number of weeks/months):

Project description:
- How the project and curricular goals match mutual needs
- Overview of the processes and strategies followed
- Summary of the organizations, schools, and issues involved

Background
- Larger context of related issues
- Community partner needs
- How the project evolved

Timeline
- Target dates and detailed description of the steps involved in completing the project
- Account of when the steps were actually completed

Project team member roles
- Students
- Teachers
- Community partners
- Community mapping support staff

Project and skills development activities
- More detailed account of what the students did to prepare for the project
  - How the students organized (teamwork) to carry out the project
  - Lesson plans and teaching tools used
  - Activities led by community mentors

Outcomes
- Interim and final products
- Benefits to students, teachers, and community partners
- Academic standards met
- Secretary's Commission on Assessing Needed Skills (SCANS) competencies met
- Student internships
- Policy changes related to project

Assessments
- Tools for assessing students: rubrics, sample tests, writing samples, project assessment, feedback from students, feedback from teachers, feedback from community partners, lessons learned, placed-based project evaluation instruments

Postscripts
- Postproject actions
- Plans for continuation of project
- Continued information sharing
- Future applications and needs of community partner

Additional resources
- Bibliography of information sources: periodicals, books, Web sites, videos, databases, surveys, and so forth
- Listing of other contacts consulted: subject matter experts, government officials, and so on

Closure and evaluation

The closing each year of CM projects is a phase just as important as the work that has preceded it, whether you plan to build on your current project or tackle an entirely new issue. The questions you ask will go a long way towards determining the course and outcome of whatever sort of work you plan to do in the future: *What did you learn from the recent experience that would help make the next one more efficient or rewarding? How might you better utilize available resources and apply mapping technology? Could academic standards be addressed more comprehensively or effectively?*

This section will briefly address two levels of evaluation from the standpoint of identifying and applying lessons learned to future CM projects:

- Individual student achievement
- Overall project success

Reality-based assessment of student achievement

Periodically during the course of the CM project, educators should conduct formative assessments of student work based on rubrics, contracts, course outlines with deliverables, and other project management directives. The results of these earlier assessments would then be factored into the final summative assessment of student achievement. At the same time, it is advisable to evaluate the formative assessments applied—did they effectively capture essential performance and provide students with timely redirection? If you did not anticipate that emphasizing good teamwork would be an important factor the first year, for example, but now realize its value to the final outcome, you will want to incorporate this criterion into future rubrics and formative assessments. You will also want to share this discovery with other educators just starting out so they can anticipate the need to emphasize teamwork at the outset, rather than learn the hard way as you did.

ACTIVITY	3 EXCELLENT	2 ACCEPTABLE	1 UNACCEPTABLE
Works effectively with mentor(s)			
Effective speaking skills			
Organizes project tasks			
Attention to quality of data collected			
Demonstrates GIS skills			
Demonstrates leadership skills			

Excerpt from a scoring rubric showing real-world entries

The CMP model assumes that educators generally know how to assess student work in the traditional sense. Assessing student work tied to community–school collaborative projects inherently involves a much more creative approach that reflects the dynamic and reality-based projects they undertake. For example, a traditional scoring rubric could still be applied, but new place-based types of activities will need to be depicted. For purposes of example, the scoring rubric above omits traditional skills and activities in order to highlight potential real-world entries.

"We used multiple tools—written work, oral presentations, and computer skills with a PowerPoint® presentation—to assess student work."

VERMONT SCHOOL TEACHER AND CMP PROJECT TEAM MEMBER

Another practical student evaluation method uses the more public platform of the project informational meetings and final presentations. Educators, project mentors, and randomly selected audience members can be enlisted to assess student presentations on a variety of relevant performance criteria using a standard format, much like the scoring rubric above. Public gatherings can also be a great venue for facilitating group evaluative discussions on a range of enlightening topics. Brainstorming indicators of success or failure can be a valuable exercise—if it is kept in a positive light. A good facilitator can lead a productive discussion about each project by using an approach depicted by the chart below:

DISCUSSION TOPICS	COMMUNITY PERSPECTIVE	EDUCATOR PERSPECTIVE	STUDENT PERSPECTIVE
A Identify the criteria and conditions that define project success.*			
B How well were the criteria and conditions met?			
C How can we advance the CM project approach to become more systemic in schools?			
D How can we better measure the effects of CM project work on student achievement?			
E What actions and strategies should be enhanced for achieving best possible outcomes in the future?			
F Who else in the school system and community should be included in the future? Why?			
G What are the next steps for continuing this CM project or building on it?			

* Examples include: Timely completion of components or tasks, effective presentation and delivery, academic standards met, student learning achieved, steady levels of enthusiasm, public recognition, pride in outcome, teamwork at all levels, respect at all levels, high-quality product, community partner uses product, continued support by organizations and school administrators, mastery of technical skills, products enhanced the understanding of the issues under investigation.

"It takes time to implement technological change."

SARAH WITHAM BEDNARZ
IMPACT AND SUCCESS: EVALUATING A GIS TRAINING INSTITUTE

Evaluating overall project success

You may already have some general guidelines on hand for evaluating the success of your project if you applied the CM project conceptualization planner (page 32) in the course of developing your project plan. One of the questions the planner posed was "What does success look like from each partner's perspective?" Your collective answers to this question effectively established your vision and goals for the outcome of your project. *Now that your project has been completed, did you accomplish these goals? Did any of them change? Does the end result resemble the shared vision?*

Through a collaborative effort, The Orton Family Foundation and a number of renowned organizations and professionals in the field of place-based evaluations have developed a series of project evaluation surveys and methods intended to standardize the collection and consolidation of data across projects. These formal tools are available to CM project teams desiring a more thorough, comprehensive evaluation of project success from multiple perspectives: educators, students, and community members. Ultimately, through the assimilation of results from numerous evaluations, the CMP model will be able to impart qualitative and quantitative evidence of student learning and program success directly related to CM projects. This broad-based, coordinated approach to project evaluation will:

- assess the effectiveness of the CMP model in terms of process
- assess the effectiveness of the CMP model in terms of outcomes
- provide useful information to aid further program development, justification, and refinement

The development of standardized assessment methods is a painstaking process, as is the administration of the surveys and the compilation of statistically valid results. The following list denotes principles of alternative assessments that are particularly applicable to place-based education and the CMP model.

- The assessment must reflect what is considered as valuable outcomes of the educational process.

- Assessment tasks should resemble, or be, real-life, problem-solving activities.

- Trustworthiness of the evaluation of the performance assessments depends on specifying and making public the criteria for quality performances, relying on multiple sources of student work, and using multiple evaluators practiced in the methods of assessment.

- Assessment information can be used to improve learning and teaching.

- The audience for whom the various assessment tasks are designed should be as real as possible.

For isolated or remote CM project teams that do not wish to become initially involved in these type of formal assessments, the following tables summarize useful background information and fundamental project evaluation questions that are easily addressed and known to spawn very useful, enlightening responses.

PROJECT BACKGROUND

- Academic standards met and others that could be met
- Logistical issues encountered
- Student advice and feedback
- Flowchart of organizational skills, project management, and mentor relationships
- Skills and tasks carried out by students—what they actually learned and did
- GIS support required
- Educator support required
- Project mentor support required
- Support required from subject-matter experts
- School and class schedules
- Project overview, criteria, products, and expectations
- Time spent on projects (by tasks)
- Samples of student work
- Case studies by project—could entail descriptive writing by students for credit
- Final evaluations

EVALUATIVE QUESTIONS

A way to gain insights about project dynamics and effectiveness
- What did you learn?
- Did you enjoy working on the project? What did you enjoy the most?
- What aspects were the most challenging?
- What was it like to work with community mentors (or students)?
- How would you do things differently if you could do the project over?
- What contributions do you feel your project team made to the community?
- How did you *(insert a specific task they accomplished)*?
- What conditions would have helped you complete your project more efficiently or effectively?
- How has this project changed your perspective on *(insert topic)*?
- What recommendations would you make to resolve the *(insert issue)* issue or problem?
- How well were your expectations met?
- Would you recommend a CM project for other students? educators? community partners? Why?

Expressing appreciation

It may go without saying, but not without great emphasis, that time must be taken at the end of each project to recognize the perseverance, loyalty, and enthusiasm of each member of a project team. Everyone must be made to feel that they contributed to the project in their own special way. An agenda item during the final public gathering or presentation, entitled Celebration Time or Appreciation Awards, could be announced in advance so that individuals can be prepared to express their gratitude to others in creative and memorable ways. Invite the media as well, as their presence can expand the audience and consequently amplify and deepen the sense of reward, recognition, and satisfaction.

Community partners have been particularly creative in recognizing school cooperation by awarding team trophies, trips, organizational products, and project publicity, either on their own or with a little coaxing. An overnight bus or plane trip to present the project to a distant audience or at a fun conference has made extraordinary impacts on students and teachers alike. Similarly, students have pitched in to buy their project mentor special thank-you gifts and present them publicly. The bottom line is to simply recognize everyone's support, even if with a simple, sincere thank you.

Behind-the-scenes supporters should also be remembered. *Who paved the way for the project in the school, partner organization or local government? Did your local journalist's coverage of the project facilitate public acceptance?* Take an ad out in the paper and thank these individuals and groups profusely!

Teachers, mentors, and students are mutually dependent in a CM project, and care should be taken to ensure each player's part is gratefully acknowledged.

*"The significant problems we face cannot be solved at the same
level of thinking we were at when we created them."*

ALBERT EINSTEIN

Part 3

How to Start a Community Mapping Program

Stepping back to observe the collective nature of multiple Community Mapping projects being conducted in proximity to each other is like viewing a community from a wide-angle lens. A new kind of community profile begins to emerge out of the spectrum of issues under investigation, more colorful and compelling than before—the result of many young and fresh perspectives working with experienced ones.

This section addresses how to a create an organized, locally-based Community Mapping program that can facilitate all phases of CM projects—from conceptualization to delivery—and coordinate training and support for a multischool, multipartner program of opportunities. It is more about pooling resources and integrating a CMP into the fabric of your community operations than it is about starting from ground zero. Our growing base of knowledge and experience will enable you to begin the start-up process at a higher level and proceed more quickly to program implementation. The Orton Family Foundation and

its expanding network of partners also have much to offer in terms of tools, training, and programmatic support to assist you, beyond the concepts set forth here. Establishing the right foundation for generating interest in and support of an innovative program is an important element in the quest for its ultimate sustainability in any community.

The ability of a central entity, the CMP staff, to guide CM project teams (students, educators, and a community partner) to success by supporting educators and promoting the sharing of ideas, resources, and experiences is fundamental to the CMP model. The CMP staff component may not be vital for conducting isolated CM projects, but it is essential for launching an effective, integrated Community Mapping program that encompasses an extensive set of participants, supporting partners, real projects, and real benefits, including a formal evaluation process.

Community Continues Work

Final Community Discussion
Final Products

Draft Products

Educators
Link ideas & needs
Enable action
Guide learning

Public Forums
Reiteration
Analysis
Field Work

Community Mapping Program Staff
Nurture local capacity
Provide tools
Provide support
Provide training

Skills Development
Team Development
Training and Tools Acquisition

Students
Relevant learning
Apply new skills
Community participation
Gain confidence

Community Partner
Mentors & role models
Subject matter experts
Link to real issues
Public mission

Standards/Assessment Planning
Product ID/ Timeline Establishment
Project Planning
Resource Identification

Community Assessment

Growing A Community Mapping Project

Supporting CM project teams

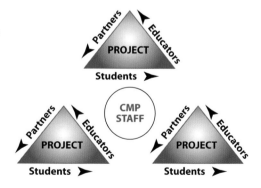

Educators who have not had prior experience leading place-based educational projects or introducing a new technology may be initially uncomfortable at the prospect of having to juggle too many new tools and teaching approaches. This is where access to outside professional support can be a valuable option for project teams. Imagine being able to call upon one or more individuals to provide your project team with GIS or place-based curriculum development assistance when you need it. Would you tackle a community-based project if you knew an outside coordinator would help you handle logistics, anticipate needs, and generally facilitate each phase of your CM project? Such a CM support team—or CMP staff—can provide educators with the back-up they need to confidently and effectively introduce a CM project and necessary skills to their students.

CM project teams are likely to produce more complex GIS products if they have ongoing access to technical support, at least during their first few CM projects.

We have found that educators with no prior GIS experience or training can also carry out rewarding CM projects if they have the support of a patient CMP staff. Such a staff must be willing to spend a little extra time leading the process on somewhat of a fast track and preparing more of the technical components for the project team instead of with them. This is one way, however, to effectively expand the local program and set the stage for these new participants to attend a CM workshop in order to take their project to the next level. Another excellent variation on this scenario is to match a CM-trained educator with an untrained one, which reduces the level of CMP staff support required and gradually draws in other interested educators.

Similarly, community partners not yet familiar with GIS—but eager to learn how it might help them—should not be discounted as possible project mentors. Given a demonstration of how GIS could address their needs and an understanding of the GIS capacity of various age groups—which CMP staff can offer—potential partners with no prior GIS experience can form realistic expectations that will enable the formation of a viable project team and the execution of a rewarding CM project.

A Community Mapping project is, on one level, an exercise in developing and sustaining relationships.

In part 2 of this book we shared two scenarios for how individual CM project ideas might evolve among community members and CM-trained educators. Similarly, in the context of an established Community Mapping program, CMP staff members are available to facilitate the initial formation of project ideas and teams as in the following scenario.

CMP staff facilitates a match

The CMP staff was familiar with the needs of a variety of community organizations, agencies, and businesses by periodically communicating with them and keeping abreast of local issues. It also remained alert to academic trends and the challenges local schools faced in meeting state standards. Recognizing a potential CM project following the release of new census data and the town's ensuing desire to assess the economic significance of the population increase, CMP staff arranged a meeting among various high school teachers, the superintendent of schools, a few town and county planners, and a Chamber of Commerce representative to explore collaborative possibilities. The group agreed that, with support from CMP staff, the marketing and math classes would form several interdisciplinary teams and use GIS to uncover specific demographic and economic changes over the past twenty years, such as population, school enrollment, unemployment rate, sales tax revenue, income, and housing costs for both the town and the county. Their results would be maintained in the town's GIS and published in a chamber brochure. The students would design the brochure using maps, charts, photos, and written summaries of the trends they discovered. Town and county planners would also use the information to forecast future trends, conceivably as other mapping projects.

The CMP staff: Coordinating a Community Mapping program

What is involved in coordinating a Community Mapping program? What is the role of the CMP staff? We will examine these questions first in order to lay the groundwork for determining who should be recruited to launch and then lead the process at a programmatic, operational level. Starting a Community Mapping program is, indeed, a process. It is a process of developing and sustaining relationships, agreements, goals, and reasons for celebrating the shared achievements of communities and institutions of learning. The CMP staff, which generally consists of one or more people from a local establishment, such as an education outreach organization, initiative, or institution, facilitates the process and provides the following overall support to participating project teams within a defined scope and region:

- project level
  - logistics coordination
  - project management and administration
- technical support
  - GIS and project design and implementation
  - curriculum development and student assessment

As a CMP matures and grows from a few projects to many, another layer of assistance and oversight may be called for:

- program management

At this more developed stage, the CMP staff would also recruit and coordinate the support of additional partners that could contribute financial resources, information and data, equipment, technical expertise, and other needed resources in a timely and systemic manner.

The goal is to bring the necessary expertise together in a cost-efficient framework of operation that is responsive to the changing needs of the program. It is not only prudent, but our strong recommendation, to build CMP staff capacity into established educational programs rather than to create a dedicated organization from scratch. A multiskilled individual may be able to initially provide both logistics coordination and technical support to a handful of CM project teams, but the quality of support is likely to decline as the number of projects increase. As needs, resources, skills, and personnel are adjusted over time, it is possible that certain responsibilities could shift to new individuals. For example, if school technology coordinators continued to sharpen their GIS skills, they might be able to provide more in-house technical support to CM project teams, thereby decreasing the need for CMP staff support and corresponding costs. This type of systemic change represents the ideal long-term scenario, where schools become increasingly less dependent on CMP staff to sustain CM project work within their communities.

The following list describes the full range of roles and programmatic responsibilities CMP staff may assume, depending on the stage of program development and the ambitions of its participants:

Program management level

- Lead the CMP development process
- Stimulate community thinking on suitable project needs and ideas
- Develop other operational partnerships
- Coordinate needs and share resources, information, and strategies with other CMPs
- Define the scope and region involved
- Maintain a CMP staff commensurate with needs
- Provide, facilitate, or secure necessary funding
- Promote place-based education
- Promote school–community partnerships through CM projects

CMP staff need to coordinate the work of students . . .

- Showcase project information and products via a Web site (such as *www.communitymap.org*)
- Provide overall guidance and support to CMP project coordinator(s)
- Expand circle of support and participation to include citizens, parents, school administrators, students, alternative learning programs, colleges, community leaders, organizations, and businesses
- Lead ongoing program evaluations, enhancements, and refinement
- Coordinate summer workshops and training opportunities and recruit participants
- Support program transferability, and document the process and experiences for purpose of sharing
- Foster communication and information sharing at all levels
- Share CMP experiences at conferences and public events

Project coordination level

- Link youth, educators, and communities through CM projects—facilitate dynamic relationships
- Support CM project design, implementation, and management
- Assist educators with integrating CM projects into curricula and with project documentation
- Serve as clearinghouse for needed resources including people, places, equipment, and data

- Provide logistical support; for example, line up transportation, training, authorizations, equipment, and media coverage
- Seek and administer necessary funding and grants for training and operations
- Visit schools and learning centers as needed to support team efforts, GIS or GPS tasks, and generation of needed map products, troubleshoot problems, facilitate progress, and document activities
- Facilitate project efficiency
- Provide incentives for educator training, participation, and project documentation tasks
- Facilitate communication among community partners, educators, and students throughout the project
- Provide information sharing opportunities among other CM project teams, educators, school administrators, organizations, and the public
- Support project teams as they prepare for and deliver public presentations
- Share CM project experiences at conferences and public events
- Keep Web site coverage of CM projects current
- Coordinate student and project assessments, both ongoing and final
- Initiate celebration of success

Technical level

- Train-the-trainer, project-based GIS instruction
- Provide initial CM training; for example, CM workshops for educators
- Coach project teams on how GIS, GPS, and other mapping and decision-making tools can be applied to specific issues and situations
- Assist educators with introduction of GIS to students in the classroom
- Gather base map data and prepare base maps for project teams
- Assist with project design, especially keeping scope small from a technical standpoint
- Help educators prepare students for data collection and field work
- Support data collection efforts in the field
- Maintain current versions of students' GIS projects, including master, interim, and final products
- Package final digital GIS products for dissemination to participating educators and community mentors at the end of the school year

. . . the work of educators and mentors.

- Help project teams prepare for and deliver presentations and convey to the audience the technical capabilities of students, including noteworthy accomplishments and challenges
- Help generate paper map plots as required by the community partner or project team
- Work closely with other CMP staff members—communicate status, needs, milestones, and so forth
- Over time the duties of the GIS specialist may be transferred to a school technology coordinator or volunteer from the community who can provide the necessary technical support

- Facilitate project evaluation discussions
- Administer or facilitate standardized student learning and achievement evaluations
- Administer or facilitate standardized final project evaluations
- Feed results of student and project evaluations into national data pool
- Help document challenges, successes, and results from academic perspective
- Work closely with other CMP staff members to communicate status, needs, and milestones.
- Represent the local CMP at appropriate conferences and workshops

Educational level

- Curriculum development, student assessment, and project evaluation
- Train educators on place-based educational concepts and approaches
- Train educators on principles of education for sustainability
- Provide new perspectives and methods for integrating real-world projects into curricula
- Provide project design and management training and guidance
- Provide student and project assessment tools and training, both summative and formative
- Promote interdisciplinary approaches to CM project execution
- Help educate community members and partners on academic standards and goals

Core CMP staff members are generally paid to coordinate the interests and support of all the partners and participants. This dedicated attention ensures the continuity and integrity of the program, minimizes the duplication of efforts, and establishes a strong platform of cooperation that may attract grants and other capital. The organization or institution that takes on a CMP can fill CMP staff positions in a variety and combination of ways:

1 Allocate existing employees to the positions.

2 Contract with individual consultants and specialists.

3 Secure additional funds to create new CMP staff positions or to hire consultants.

4 Engage dependable, committed volunteers (who may eventually become paid CMP staff members).

While CMP staff positions are generally linked to one organization, they may be dispersed across several. Staff member duties also are malleable enough to form around available strengths and expertise. For example, it is entirely possible that one person could provide both project coordination and curriculum development support, or program management and technical support, depending on the number of project teams involved and the extent of support they have been promised. As the number of teams increase over time, it may be necessary to also grow the CMP staff and recruit additional partners and experts in order to maintain the same level of support.

We have found that many CM project teams may have neither the time nor the desire to coordinate needs, resources, and logistics within their own project, and consequently depend on CMP staff to fulfill these functions. Similarly, while they welcome opportunities to share information and experiences with other project teams, they generally do not want to be involved in planning such gatherings. This tendency further validates the leadership role that CMP staff members play in perpetuating the most effective CMP implementation process for a given mix of participants at various phases of program development.

The process of starting and maintaining a Community Mapping program follows a similar pattern as that described in part 2 for initiating CM projects. It naturally involves more people and requires more resources to assimilate all the pieces into an integral program with common goals. A CMP can systematically grow out of a few pilot projects or it can be launched as a full program by a dedicated CMP staff. In the latter case, CMP staff would take the lead in building initial support at both the programmatic and project levels and engaging a diverse group of partners and participants in the mobilization process. Overlaps will invariably occur among individuals and organizations involved in the development of a CMP and associated CM projects. This is a very desirable outcome as it reinforces the relationships that provide continuity between both operational levels.

As facilitated by CMP staff, your program development process will likely be more dynamic than the linear path represented here. Regardless of the sequence of events you expect to follow, you will want to consider each of the core tasks depicted below at the outset, during the exploratory and planning phases of your CMP. It is as important to plan training and project implementation strategies early, for example, as it is to build the operational framework of your CMP. Anticipating future needs at the project level and being able to adequately address them is critical to the success of the program as a whole.

Starting and sustaining a CMP is a process that entails the fundamental tasks outlined below. The role of the CMP staff is to lead and facilitate this process and these tasks, in a logical order that is tailored to the dynamics of the community or region being served. The CMP staff, by virtue of their own mission and reach, will have broadly defined a scope and region of interest before embarking on the following journey, knowing these factors are subject to change as the process unfolds.

I   Assess community readiness

II   Recruit and organize local resources

III   Establish a common mission

IV   Conceptualize your program model

V   Draft an initial budget

VI   Recruit project ideas and project teams

VII   Provide training

VIII   Implement and support projects

IX   Share results and experiences

X   Assess student achievement, project success, and program effectiveness

I. Assess community readiness

Readiness denotes willingness and capacity. Assessing a community's readiness is a fairly straightforward task that serves to answer the overriding question: *What needs can the CMP address, what resources are available, and what is the potential level of interest in the program?* More specifically, this task can be broken down as follows:

- Identify potential partners and participants
  Who would care?
  - Be open to all age groups, professions, organizations, academic institutions, and educational initiatives
- Assess the technical capacity of the community, schools, and alternative learning programs
  - Access to computers and GIS software
  - Computer competency
  - GIS software experience
  - GIS training experience

- Spread the word
  - Share ideas and existing success stories
  - Network, network, and network
  - Engage the media in helping to publicize the program and organizational meetings
- Identify needs and key issues
  - *What equipment, data, and software do we need?*
  - *What do we need to understand or investigate?*
  - *What issues could be addressed collaboratively by communities and schools?*
  - *How would a mapping component enhance collaborative investigations?*
  - *What historical information do we need to gather, preserve, and graphically represent?*
  - *How can we further promote a sense of place by working together and engaging our young people?*

Bringing different types of partners together requires mutually educating each other on respective needs, interests, and vernacular. Community partners and educators who mentor students at the project level should exemplify effective communication as it pertains to their CMP project and related course work.

- Start building a common vision
  - Brainstorm possibilities for projects and project teams (as outlined in part 2)
- Bring potential partners together to explore roles and directions
  Who will provide what kind of support?
  - Program-level (funding, leadership, specialists, resources, sharing)
  - Project-level (logistics, access to resources, design, and implementation support)
  - Technical (mapping, GIS, curriculum development, project management, assessment)
  - Educational (student skills, academic standards, mentoring, school administrative support)
- Determine the next steps
  What shall we try to accomplish by when?
  - Immediate
  - Short term
  - Long term

Importantly, the activities involved in this first task provide the basis for creating a shared, or collaborative vision. Creating a shared vision compels people to take a stand for a preferred future and defines an image of a desired end state. *What does success look like? What will the CMP look like in three or five years? In ten or twenty years? What are the steps involved in getting there?*

Readiness objective
Identify needs, resources, and initial vision

II. Recruit and organize local resources

This task involves enlisting stakeholders and identifying the assets they have to offer. The stakeholders include individuals, community organizations, school representatives, educators, and youth identified earlier in response to the questions *Who cares?* and *Who would provide the necessary support?* The needs and guiding vision expressed in the previous task should drive the pooling and organization of resources that are germane to the program at various levels, including the programmatic, project, technical, and educational levels.

Types of resources and commitments to recruit include:

- existing CMP model designs and approaches
- representatives of applicable professions and agencies
- potential project-level participants (community partners, educators, and youth)
- equipment
- services
- software
- data and information
- lesson plans and curricula
- funding

Since needed resources are best found through networking, this iterative task has the potential to draw a very large group of stakeholders. A highly recommended and advantageous action is to establish a smaller CMP advisory group (roughly fifteen individuals) that best represents the diverse interests of the larger group. The advisory group will be better able to lead a more efficient process of gathering and organizing available resources, reaching consensus, and moving the development of the CMP forward systematically. To be successful, it should support a dynamic composition of local and even regional representatives that vary with the evolving character of the CMP.

> **Recruiting objective**
> *Gather resource commitments*

III. Establish a common mission

Building on the initial CMP vision, the next process of developing a common mission can be powerful and unifying and can serve as the rallying point for greater collaboration and participation. Below are some strategies for establishing a common mission. These would ideally emerge from brainstorming sessions facilitated by CMP staff that involved interested stakeholders, or at a minimum, the CMP advisory group. These discussions will invariably spark the need to bring in additional resources and individuals not yet drawn into the process.

A *Evaluate the local climate* (conduct a SWOT Analysis)
  1 Strengths
  2 Weaknesses
  3 Opportunities
  4 Threats

B *Assess big-picture perspectives*
  1 Audiences served
  2 Hopes
  3 Fears
  4 Needs
  5 Benefits
  6 Constraints and limitations
  7 Flexibilities

C *Other initial considerations*
  1 Existing knowledge base and skills of teachers and students
  2 Training needs: technical and non-technical; educators and students
  3 Ability to integrate a CM project into existing curricula

  4 Academic standards and educational goals that need to be met
  5 Community understanding of academic standards and their role
  6 Level of place-based, inquiry-based, or project-based education in schools
  7 Level of experience relating to service learning and school–community efforts
  8 Relevant and accessible local funding resources
  9 Timing and schedules

D *Adopt a common language*

Consider the various sectors and interests represented in both the CMP and project team environments, such as academic, professional, business, nonprofit, and government, and have them each explicitly commit to adopting commonly understood language and terminology. If certain distinctive terms, concepts, and acronyms are unavoidable, make sure that everyone clearly understands their meaning and respects their intent.

Examples of terms that may need to be retained and explained often stem from technology and academia, for example: GIS/GPS, themes, database, rubric, academic standards, place-based education, and spatial relationships. Non-academicians would probably appreciate simple translations of terms often used in public school systems, like formative and summative assessments. They would also benefit from a basic understanding of what academic standards are, what their role is, how important they are to the public educational process, and which academic standards apply to their CM project. Community specialists and "-ologists" also have distinctive vocabularies that may surface at the project level and cause confusion, unless they are prepared to either translate their expressions to educators and students or make a concerted effort to speak in simple and clear terms from the outset.

E *Define the specific benefits to be derived*

Invariably newcomers to the CMP will ask *What's in it for me?* Anticipating this question and being prepared to share specific incentives and benefits of the CMP is paramount to securing support and committed partners. What kinds of meaningful benefits will the following sectors (i.e., audiences served) realize by participating in or supporting CM efforts at one or more levels? Consider both the tangible and intangible benefits.

1 Whole community or region

2 Community partners and mentors

3 Schools and school districts

4 School administrators

5 Educators

6 Students

7 Parents

8 Other

Will the benefits gained be justified by the commitments offered, and how important is that? Brainstorming the potential benefits of a CMP in a group setting is a valuable exercise that can draw additional partners to the table. Certainly the documented benefits realized by existing CMPs should be taken into consideration, as these results can validate the expectations of new partners. This information can help address the question *Are my expectations realistic?*

Preparing a simple handout that summarizes the CMP vision and respective benefits is another way to provoke interest among prospective partners and participants. This document should be treated as a work in progress and periodically updated. Following are examples of typical benefits students and community partners might realize that could be included in such a handout.

STUDENT BENEFITS
- Experiential learning opportunities.
- Leadership and negotiation skills.
- Applied teamwork.
- Listening, critical-thinking, and decision-making skills.
- Mapping and technical skills.
- Data collection, analysis, and interpretation skills.
- Practice organizing information.
- Time management and project management skills.
- Communication and public presentation skills.
- Experience community involvement.
- Exposure to the professional world and different career options.

EDUCATOR BENEFITS
- Projects help students meet academic standards in new and creative ways.
- Relevant, hands-on, interdisciplinary teaching helps motivate students to learn and achieve.
- Educators and students build relationships through connections with other CM project teams.
- Recognition for contributing to a "sense of place."
- Recognition for community involvement, academic achievements, and innovation.

COMMUNITY AND COMMUNITY PARTNER BENEFITS
- Receive products of value produced by students.
- New data, information, and GIS input gained.
- Organizational education outreach efforts more effective.
- Public awareness of the organization and its mission strengthened.
- Citizen participation in public meetings improved.

SAMPLE MISSION STATEMENTS

The Orton Family Foundation seeks to help citizens of all ages define the future, shape the growth, and preserve the heritage of their communities.
- We develop and deliver innovative community land-use planning tools and processes.
- We facilitate citizen participation in defining their communities' future.
- We provide education, training, and information resources to professional planners, community leaders, and citizens to more effectively manage growth.

The Yampa Valley Community Mapping Program connects students with resources and opportunities that create working relationships with communities, explore real issues firsthand, and contribute spatial products that enhance their and our understanding of Yampa Valley's heritage and sense of place.

F *Draft a program mission statement*

The above steps should lead to the collaborative crafting of a CMP mission statement that reflects or directly includes the group vision.

A mission statement addresses:

- Who you are
- What you do
- Who you serve
- To what end

G *Adopt guiding principles*

Defining guiding principles for your Community Mapping Program is central to building appropriate expectations and continuity across projects. *What fundamental values will lead to program and project-level success? What common elements and goals of your CMP must project teams subscribe to in order to justify dedicated programmatic support? What doctrines characterize the heart and spirit of your Community Mapping Program?*

We recommend considering how The Orton Family Foundation's Guiding Principles can be adapted to your local or regional interests. The process of evaluating principles that have been found to work elsewhere will foster confidence among project-level participants and common ground among operational partners. These principles are listed below and defined at the front of this book.

- Community needs
- Connections and continuity
- Place-based learning
- Visualization and technology
- Sharing results
- Reflection and assessment

Common mission objective
Assimilate program guidelines

IV. Conceptualize your program model

Creating a graphic portrayal of your program model early in the development process forces interested partners to define their supporting relationships at both the programmatic and project levels. This type of model diagram is also very useful in recruiting other partners, project-level resources, and financial support for your program because it conveys broad-based collaboration; it is therefore a good idea to keep the model current so that it reflects the CMP's evolving nature, vision, and growing base of operational resources. *Who should lead the task of creating and maintaining the program model?* Typically CMP staff members, the CMP advisory group, a newly appointed program coordinator or manager, and other individuals who have the desire and experience to tackle this task in a visually effective and graphic manner.

A CMP often forms around the mission of the principle organization leading its development. For example, an environmental education outreach organization may target a specific region, state, or set of school districts. Other organizations may focus on a central theme of investigation, like historical preservation or geography education. Depending on the nature and growing complexity of your CMP, you may eventually want to construct more detailed conceptual models (including tables, charts, matrices, flowcharts, or GIS maps) of project-level operations, such as:

- region served (school districts, communities, valley)

- central theme (current issues, watershed, water quality, fire mitigation, homeland security, community service, natural resources, recreation, agriculture)

- matrix of needs expressed by schools

- matrix of issues expressed by community organizations

- project ideas

- project sites

- project development and implementation process

- sources of project-level resources

- interrelationships of various project teams

- timeline of events

Prospective financial partners may appreciate graphic depictions of how their support will enhance or grow the

Guiding principles, a consice statement of mission, and clear goals are the foundation, armature, and vision of a CM project.

model. Similarly, CM program coordinators should consider creating detailed databases for tracking and then matching project-level needs, resources, and partners. Databases can serve as powerful clearinghouse tools to coordinate the information collected on the previously mentioned "Project Description Forms" submitted by community partners and the "Educator Needs Forms" filled out by educators (see appendix).

The Colorado CMP advisory group identified the need for and then developed a comprehensive flowchart of the project development process as a planning tool for new CM project teams. This six-foot-tall flowchart has since become the basis for the project design, management, and assessment training offered as an integral part of The Orton Family Foundation's CMP. Importantly, the advisory group was comprised of community and school partners and CMP staff members, representing a broad cross section of interests and expertise.

> **Modeling objective**
> *Map relationships among program elements*

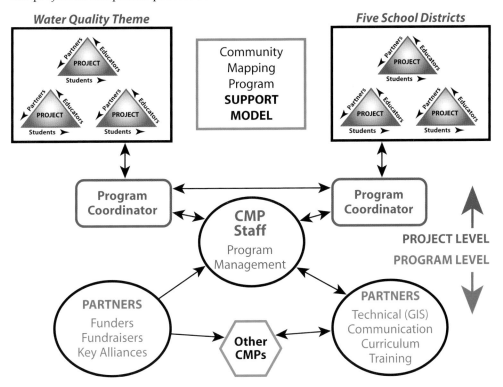

V. Draft an initial budget

Throughout the conceptualization and planning process of your Community Mapping program you will want to make note of possible funding needs related to both your short- and long-term vision and goals. Of course, whatever resources you can borrow or have donated could substantially reduce the capital required. We have experienced a tremendous sharing of resources at the project level and a greater need to secure funding for program administration and formal training. Keeping costs on a shoestring budget at first, and gradually accumulating additional resources as the program grows certainly warrants careful consideration.

Concentrate on building a track record of small project successes. Then use your growing success to attract additional resources, funding, and operational partners. This methodical approach fosters greater loyalty and support from your current partners—which you want to keep—and a solid base for expanding the depth, breadth, and fiscal support of your program.

Both the Yampa Valley Community Mapping Program in Colorado and the Vermont Institute of Natural Science sought outside grants the first few years to help defray the program-level costs that were largely covered by The Orton Family Foundation. As expected, the gradual addition of new project teams resulted in a greater proportion of outside funds being directed to training educators and providing technical project support in the second year. Additional funds were secured by the Colorado CMP in year two to train five school technology coordinators in advanced GIS as a way to begin transferring the technical support function directly to the schools. Unfortunately, due to the extraordinarily demanding nature of their jobs, the technology coordinators were never able to devote the necessary attention to new CM projects as was hoped and expected. This outcome further validated the supporting role of the outside GIS specialist in the CMP model.

Two charts in the appendix attempt to itemize a CMP start-up budget for both a low-end (simple model) and a high-end program. The high-end budget supports more project teams and builds in educator incentives and the best refreshments in copious amounts for CM workshops and subsequent public events. The chart does not cover new hardware.

Besides the projected numbers of projects and participants, your start-up and annual CMP budgets will depend on available local resources, actual needs, and commitments of financial support (including grant awards). If resources are limited, you can phase in project teams, training, equipment, and other resources. Manual mapping techniques can be an excellent substitute for GIS software, for instance, until sufficient hardware, software, and training funds are secured.

> **Budget objective**
> *Create a strategy for phasing in financial resources*

VI. Recruit project ideas and project teams

Potential project ideas and participants should have already been identified in earlier program planning and needs assessment discussions. It is natural to address *What if?* questions when envisioning how the program would manifest itself at the project level. It is also essential that project ideas emerge throughout the CMP planning process in order to draw community partners—project hosts and mentors—and educators with their students to the table.

Matching mutual needs with available resources and identifying viable projects represent the core of project-clearinghouse duties led by CMP staff each year. Involving the support of CMP staff from the outset, regardless of who identifies the project idea, will lead to the design and implementation of feasible projects—ones that are characterized by small or reasonable scopes and expectations.

If needs have not yet been identified and documented, then now is the time to promote and support this type of dedicated, project-level planning exercise. This step forces serious consideration of the possible community–school projects that might be feasible and could be enhanced by a mapping component. It also leads to promising partnerships and project teams. One way CMP staff or the advisory group can facilitate this process is by helping community members and educators fill out Project Description and Educator Needs forms (see appendix) and then use them to identify common interests. Alternatively, CMP staff may elect to develop a project application (request for proposals) form or a preworkshop packet that guides educators and

Publicist, proselytizer, prophet: CMP staffers need to energetically promote the idea of CM projects, as well as coordinate the projects themselves.

potential project teams through a project conceptualization process prior to CM training. Ideally, project ideas and teams should take shape prior to CM training, as this enables team members to apply the methodologies taught during the workshop directly to their projects.

It is helpful when recruiting new project partners to provide them with a summary of overall program goals and expectations, in addition to other needs identification documents. The needs identification process, which leads to project ideas and teams, is covered in much more detail in part 2 of this book; this early groundwork will not be fully recapped here.

Community partners appreciate knowing in advance what is expected of them in their role as mentors. How much time will they need to devote to classroom training, fieldwork, data assimilation, student skills development, product development, coordination meetings, and public presentations? Educators, on the other hand, want to hear about incentives (stipends, substitutes, graduate credits and so forth), training, technical support, and other logistics in order to feel comfortable and get excited about taking on a CM project. They want to know what is expected of them and what commitments their students may need to make. Now that your planning process has resulted in a program vision, draft budget, and project-level goals, CMP staff should be well prepared to summarize these general factors and provisions in a format that is applicable across

projects. This document provides the framework for developing a functional project agreement and timeline for deliverables later on.

In Colorado, CMP staff (program coordinator) becomes an ambassador each year from January through May, aggressively spreading the word about the CMP and upcoming presentations, coordination meetings, summer workshops, and CM project opportunities. Needs, issues, and project ideas are collected and a concerted effort is devoted to recruiting educators, as they are the hardest to reach through conventional channels. By summer, most project teams have formed and enrolled in CM workshops. CM projects will be fully designed and planned by the start of school, except for any details that can wait for student input. In Vermont, the first part of the year is also spent publicizing opportunities, guiding project conceptualization, and collecting applications from prospective project teams so that they are also ready to go when summer training and planning workshops begin.

Project recruiting objective
Match ideas and teams systematically

VII. Provide training

New CMP staff members and educators will need instruction on (1) how to introduce and use GIS in a community-based project setting, and (2) how to design and manage CM projects so they can be successfully completed and also meet community and academic expectations. It is very important for CMP staff and educators with a GIS background to attend CM training to acquire specialized tools and learn effective methodologies for accomplishing CM project objectives. Accordingly, start-up CMP schedules and budgets should allow for one of the first-year training scenarios depicted in the table on page 86, where qualified CM instructors conduct the initial CM train-the-trainers workshop. Through their newly gained understanding of how CM strategies and tools can facilitate the project development and implementation process, CMP staff will be better able to assist educators, and educators will be better prepared to guide students, back in the classroom and field. Developing an ability to anticipate and address needs and problems before they become critical is a fundamental goal of CM training.

The nature of project-based CM training is covered in more detail in other sections of this book, but is recapped here in order to reemphasize the unique approach and also to introduce a programmatic level of training and guidance for new CMP staff:

1 The CM process: more than just GIS for educators

The Community Mapping brand of GIS training emulates the process involved in carrying out a CM project. Educators and new CMP staff learn how to introduce GIS basics to their students for immediate application in real life projects—not how to master the full range of GIS capabilities. They receive an organized toolbox of GIS exercises and lessons, but more importantly, a roadmap that indicates when to use which tools. Woven into this technical training process are project design, management, and assessment tools and methodologies that assist project teams in designing and successfully integrating a community-based project into academic curricula and alternative learning programs. This track is integral to the CM process, as is the ability to anticipate the inevitable challenges. The CM process promotes the development of real-world partnerships, particularly between youth and community mentors, and emulates a client–contractor relationship in terms of meeting mutual expectations. These concepts plus the value of communicating progress through ongoing evaluations and various assessment techniques are also emphasized in CM training. It is targeted primarily at educators and, therefore, extremely important for CMP staff to fully grasp as well.

	FIRST-YEAR TRAINING OPTIONS	WHO ATTENDS	OUTCOME
1	**CM Institute** • Annual summer workshop* • Need-to-know GIS • Train-the-trainers • Project design and management • Student assessments • Project evaluations • Based on local issue and project in community where training is conducted	• New CMP staff members • Interested educator teams • Mixed group representing many diferent locations • Periodically, a community partner representing the issue	• Dynamic interactions of diverse teams learning together • Technical skills, tools, project plans, and a teaching/assessment strategy to follow for introducing GIS and the CM project to students • Sample GIS base map, data, and layout produced during training
2	**On-site CM training** • Host CMP determines time and place • Need-to-know GIS • Train-the-trainers • Project design and management • Student assessments • Project evaluations • Based on local issue and project in community where host CMP is located	• New CMP staff members • Committed educators • Periodically, a community partner representing the issue	• Dynamic interactions of CMP staff with their own project teams learning together • Technical skills, tools, project plans, and a teaching/assessment strategy to follow for introducing GIS and the CM project to students • Actual GIS base map, data, and layout that students can build on as they continue the investigation as part of the CM project team

* Visit *www.communitymap.org* for current CM Institute offerings.

2 CMP management: more than just a CD of digital tools for CMP staff and educators

While this section covers specific concepts and approaches for starting a CMP, it does not provide the full range of practical tools that have been continuously refined since 1999 for implementing these strategies. New CMP staff members and educators will acquire project-based materials during CM training that will effectively help them coordinate and guide the activities of project team members. But, why would CMP staff want to reinvent all new programmatic

tools when existing ones can be acquired and tailored to their situation?

The Orton Family Foundation and Vermont Institute of Natural Science have compiled the most useful and versatile coordination, instructional, and evaluation instruments for this purpose, as both a supplement to CM training and an aid to CMP staff, advisory groups, and educators. Importantly, the digital materials include standardized tools for evaluating CM-related impacts at the student, educator, and community levels with avenues to contribute your results to a national database and enable ongoing analyses of program effectiveness on a larger scale. Information about upcoming workshops and obtaining the latest program evaluation results will be maintained on the Foundation's community mapping Web site (*www.communitymap.org*). We will continue to update our collective CM toolbox with innovative instruments and methodologies developed by other CM ventures and strongly encourage this level of sharing in order to further inspire and support the efforts of our growing network of CM program and project teams.

Recognizing that time is often the greatest limiting factor in launching new endeavors and efficiency the greatest ambition, the Foundation and VINS can also be called upon to guide CMP staff and advisory groups in facilitating the program conceptualization and development process, application of programmatic tools (contained on the CD), training of participants, and recruitment of financial partners and resources. Additionally, partnerships may be established that would enable other CMPs to join us in teaching the CM process and similarly supporting the expansion of the CMP in their region and field of interest.

3 CM GIS day camp: more than just a GIS boot camp for youth, educators, and community members

Educators, community members, and youth become particularly motivated and adventurous when given the opportunity to explore real-world GIS applications together under the structured, but flexible guidance of a qualified instructor. Learning technological applications in an environment filled with diverse perspectives and capabilities can be especially enriching for participants. This introductory, project-based GIS workshop is targeted at the end user—not instructors or educators—and is a great way to provide curious individuals of all ages the opportunity to test-drive a fun, new tool. CM GIS day camps, which are five days long and scheduled during the summer, can give educators and community members valuable insight into student capacities to master GIS skills and applications. Hence, participation in a CM GIS day camp often leads to enrollment in the train-the-trainers CM workshop and enthusiastic involvement in CM projects.

Training objective
Match training options to participant needs and preferences

VIII. Implement and support projects

As emphasized in a previous section, the key to implementing CM projects is ongoing communication. CMP staff can play a huge role in fueling timely contacts within project teams and beyond.

Get students in the field right away. Immerse students in the feel of their site as soon as possible—whether it is an outdoor field site, a museum archive, or an art studio—get them out of their classrooms!

They can also monitor progress, anticipate obstacles, and head off crises or project abandonment with timely leadership or intervention.

How do you initially inform, motivate, and engage students in a CM project? Most educators invite the primary community partner (mentor) to their class at the very beginning to explain the mission directly to students from their perspective—the why, what, how, when, where, and who aspects of the project. Educators then complement the discussion by reviewing how the project fits into their coursework, what avenues students have to help develop the project plan and pursue tasks of special interest, what they will learn, and how they will be assessed. Students should be allowed plenty of time for questions and discussion and encouraged to contribute their own ideas.

Another important early implementation step is to introduce GIS, GPS, and relevant mapping technologies to students early in the project to enable them to grasp the concepts and creatively apply the tools to their tasks. CMP staff should be involved in this process, ideally providing back-up support, but also acting as the lead instructor as warranted. Part 2 of this book covers the approach for introducing GIS technologies to students in more detail. (Notably, CM training specifically prepares educators to be the lead GIS instructor.)

Keeping the momentum going during project implementation is another important job for CMP staff. Often the simple gestures of inviting local reporters to various project-related events can result in timely publicity that also serves to validate the students' work. Anticipating and tackling project resource needs is always a valued service CMP staff can fulfill, as well as keeping school administrators aware of the initiatives and innovations of educators and students alike. CMP staff will want to review part 2 of this book for many other insights on ways to facilitate the project implementation process and pave the way for project teams to move forward smoothly to product delivery and success.

Implementation objectives
Motivate, anticipate, facilitate, communicate, support

IX. Share results and experiences

Programmatic reasons for encouraging information sharing across CM project teams can range from broadening public awareness and support to openly recognizing project-related capabilities, achievements, and challenges of students. Guidance offered to project teams by CMP staff that is based on experienced observation does not necessarily have the same effect as it does coming from individuals who actually carry out the work—the students, educators, and community mentors themselves. Students are more apt to listen to their peers and educators to other educators than they are to an outside administrator, particularly when the participants speak from different levels of experience.

Several means for sharing results and experiences among members of an individual CM project are covered in the Dissemination and Information Sharing section of part 2, and easily apply to interteam exchanges as well. A face-to-face event allowing for student presentations and interactions is particularly effective for project teams within close enough proximity to convene at a central location. Such a gathering may be called a review meeting, open house, roundtable, or any name the project teams collectively choose. Video-conferencing can also be used to facilitate an all-inclusive process rather than one that benefits only a few teams within an extensive program area. One year, CMP staff conducted a videoconference between the Colorado and Vermont project teams to give students from vastly distant geographic regions an opportunity to interact and compare their CM experiences.

The purpose and nature of CM project review meetings will evolve over time—within a given year and over successive years—as participants gain experience, encounter new challenges, and aspire to greater accomplishments. Typically, review meetings should provide opportunities for participating students, educators, and community mentors to:

- share early experiences (past)
- celebrate discoveries and milestones (past–present)
- apply results to local issues (present)
- troubleshoot problems and revise current project directions (present–future)
- explore possibilities for related or expanded investigations (future)

Especially during the first year when CM project experiences are just beginning to escalate, CMP staff should facilitate the scheduling of one or more project review meetings during the school year. Some important guidelines to consider include:

- Reach consensus on the number of meetings and potential dates either prior to or as early as possible in the school year; an ambitious three-meeting scenario may entail:
  – Meeting #1—within two months of school start-up (limit audience to project team members to allow students to practice speaking in a relatively safe environment)
  – Meeting #2—mid-year (expand the audience beyond project team members, including interested teachers, school administrators, and parents)
  – Meeting #3—near the end of the school year, but at least five weeks before the last day (showcase projects via a final public event—everyone invited)

  If only one review meeting is logistically feasible during the school year, it is best to schedule it after the majority of projects have been completed, generally in mid to late April, and to treat the gathering as the final public presentation (meeting #3).

- Widely publicize the final public review meeting to the entire community, using all available media (local paper, radio and television stations, Internet, letters and notices posted in strategic locations); have students lead the publicity effort as appropriate and time-permitting.

- Based on space and other limiting factors, assist educators, as needed, with the selection of a small number of students to represent their project team, perhaps as a reward for exceptional work.

- Encourage students to take a lead role in their team's presentations, with teachers and community mentor on hand to introduce and support them.

- Vary or rotate meeting locations and venues to enable different individuals to attend; select facilities that can comfortably accommodate a desired (or anticipated) audience size and presentation needs, plus offers adequate parking and refreshment staging areas.

- Budget permitting, provide generous refreshments and reimbursements to schools for substitute teachers and transportation.

- Consider teleconferencing or video-conferencing as necessary to include the more remote project teams.

- Solicit agenda items in advance, but stick to the key purpose of each review meeting.

- Document all related activities and dates leading up to and including review meetings on each project team's timeline.

CMP staff should try to vary the content of review meetings, especially if more than one is held during the same school year. The following list summarizes specific ideas and topics to consider including on the different agendas:

Initial review meeting
- Acknowledge project milestones (show 'n tell—may be more "tell" than "show").
- Determine overall status of project against the timeline.
- Determine immediate and long-term needs to complete the project.
- Consider revising project scope.
- Determine new milestones.
- Encourage student feedback.

Mid-year review meeting
- Acknowledge project accomplishments (show 'n tell—as graphic as possible).
- Identify and discuss
  –challenges
  –surprises and discoveries
  –successes
- Explore lessons learned.

Year-end review meeting and public presentation
- Acknowledge final project accomplishments and products (show 'n tell as highly graphic and as technology-based as applicable).

- Ask evaluative questions of students, educators, and mentors.
- Determine future directions of individual projects.
- Determine future training needs.
- Discuss project documentation that would be beneficial to compile for other educators and project teams considering similar ventures.
- Celebrate the outcomes, achievements, and a job well done by all project team members!

During information sharing meetings it is important to not only demonstrate student learning and technical capabilities, but also to look for recurrent themes (see the table on the next page) that might shed light on what is and what might not be working. The earlier these matters are flushed out, the greater is the chance for success by either diverting a crisis or building on victories.

We found that we could get beyond superficial (all-glowing) progress reports and into how students, educators, and mentors were really doing by facilitating separate adult and student discussion groups. Immediately following student presentations to the entire group, including a general question-and-answer period on each project, two concurrent discussion sessions would be led. Only one adult—an impartial, vibrant facilitator (not a participating educator)—would be allowed in the students' breakout room, as students tend to be more open with each other if they know their

---

RECURRENT THEMES

1   Project strengths
2   Project weaknesses
3   Logistical issues
4   Technical/technological issues
5   Confusion about roles
6   Unanticipated benefits
7   Need for additional resources (experts, equipment, funds)
8   Value of community interactions
9   Value of real-world issues
10 Value of specific resources (people, things)
11 Value of connecting project outcomes to academic standards
12 Need for more training
13 Intra- and interproject communications
14 Avenues for project publicity and access to products
15 Building longevity into the project curriculum framework
16 Building and using mapping project resources *(www.communitymap.org,* CMP staff, project documentation)

---

remarks will be kept confidential or anonymous. The facilitators of the student and adult groups keep discussions on track and record comments for review and assimilation by CMP staff with the promise of anonymity for the students. These discussions invariably generate valuable feedback and insights into needed improvements at the program and project levels.

Students and educators alike can be inspired by learning firsthand how their peers in other schools are dealing with very similar challenges and by being encouraged to help each other resolve some of the issues in a positive group setting. They can also be motivated by others' accomplishments. Possible topics to pose to the respective groups are listed below (see page 93). You will want to select a few topics either prior to the meeting or by a group selection process.

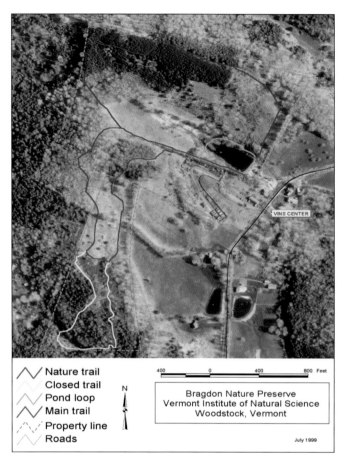

Nature trail
Closed trail
Pond loop
Main trail
Property line
Roads

400   0   400   800 Feet

N

Bragdon Nature Preserve
Vermont Institute of Natural Science
Woodstock, Vermont

July 1999

Just as GIS is designed to load data into a superficial map, CM projects load into students experiences that may otherwise be less accessible, or even impossible to come by.

In addition to the information dissemination and dynamic exchanges that occur at CMP review meetings, The Orton Family Foundation recognizes the benefit of sharing results, materials, and experiences across CMP boundaries. Exchanging materials, results, and experiences at this level will ultimately enrich the quality, potential, and effectiveness of the CMP model and CM efforts wherever they are undertaken. The avenues for sharing knowledge beyond distinct CMPs are numerous and well used by most of us already—Web sites, seminars, conferences, CM workshops, and published papers to name a few. Such media also make it possible for prospective program and project participants to explore the full range of possibilities and resources available before they embark on a similar effort and to continue drawing on the experiences of other programs as their respective CM processes advance.

Web sites are always a convenient outlet for collecting and disseminating project results, products, plans, curricula, and related information on an ongoing basis. Additionally, they provide a platform for creative or technically-inclined students to express the poignant features of their project from their perspective and for all students to chat with each other about their work, challenges, and troubleshooting efforts. Many students discover that building Web pages about their CM project is a great way to organize pertinent information prior to presenting their results to a live audience.

ADULT SESSION DISCUSSION TOPICS	STUDENT SESSION DISCUSSION TOPICS
• Who should be involved in project planning? • Should students be taught project planning? • How can we integrate multiple schools into the same CMP project? • How to enforce timelines and deadlines. • How to structure student task teams. • How much responsibility should students have for initiating communications with community partners and mentors? • How is the teachers' role working, in terms of providing student guidance, skills training, and assessment? • How is the mentor's role working? • Do students understand the difference between *planning* and *doing?* • Is GIS (or mapping technologies) truly being treated as a *tool* that enhances the curriculum and understanding of the issue? • What additional training needs have emerged? • What opportunities can we provide students for pursuing related career interests?	• Why do students want to participate in a CMP project? • What is the purpose of *place-based* education? • What is the value of working with mentors? • What do you think about integrating schools on the same project? • What do you think about bringing schools together to review their CMP projects? • What new skills have you learned? How might these skills come in handy later? • What successes have you realized? • What challenges did you face? How did you deal with them? • Did the GIS/mapping technology enhance your project? • Should students be involved in the project planning process? • How has your CMP project experience affected you personally? • Would you recommend this experience for other students? • Why?

The motivation for project teams and full programs to document student and project results should be to ultimately learn from and pass on the information—to benefit from the experiences of others and to take credit for contributing new insights on effective and rewarding practices. Stipends, graduate credits, and other incentives may be a practical way for CMP staff to encourage educators to document the process their team followed, including the tools and curricula used, and interim and final products generated. Alerting educators at the beginning of each project that certain materials will be requested upon project completion allows them to plan their documentation strategy more efficiently.

Communication among different, perhaps isolated, programs is strongly encouraged as it constantly infuses new resources into the big picture, cultivates collaboration and makes it easier for even the smallest CM ventures to find local support and funding. The Orton Family Foundation will certainly continue to facilitate communication, collaboration, and support for Community Mapping programs, wherever they materialize in the years to come.

Sharing objective
Contribute to the growing knowledge base of CMP tools and strategies

X. Assess student achievement, project success, and program effectiveness

From a program perspective, evaluative information and feedback is fundamental to continuance and growth. This information can be difficult to glean, however, without overt inducement or subtle pressure on project team members. It is equally important for students' work to be regularly evaluated, followed by timely, constructive critiques that fuel their motivation and guide them toward project success. We have found that CMP staff must often take direct measures to engage project teams in the evaluative process—both the educators and community partners can become so immersed in their projects that they do not make student and project assessment a top priority.

Further, while educators can readily factor student assessment strategies into their curricula, they may have more difficulty appraising the qualitative aspects of Community Mapping projects. *How do you assess and weigh a student's grasp of GIS technology in the context of your biology or art class? How do you grade the teamwork, communication, and leadership skills demonstrated?* While these concerns are addressed in CM training and supplemental resources, CMP staff may need to encourage and support the administration of pertinent assessments throughout the entire project, including the timely communication of feedback and direction to students.

An overview of various methods for assessing student work and project success is covered in the Closure and Evaluation section of part 2, including topics for group discussion and examination, and applicable tools are provided in CM workshop materials and the CD containing supplemental resources. Experience dictates that educators need to schedule dedicated time to plan and incorporate effective assessment tools into their course work—tools that will give them, the project mentor, and CMP staff, meaningful insights into how the project is going and what areas could be improved. Importantly, CM training provides educators with time for developing or tailoring appropriate assessment tools with experienced professionals on hand to guide the process.

CMP staff members are in an excellent position to collect anecdotes and testimonials that describe the qualitative achievements of students who have benefited in different ways as a result of their CM project work. Educators have an even better vantage point and yardstick for recognizing changes in student learning patterns and abilities and should diligently document them. Sharing student accomplishments is important in keeping parents, school administrators, and students excited about CM projects and supportive of place-based education as an effective learning practice. Community partners may also remain ready to host more CM projects when they have been publicly credited for positively affecting student achievement—but this achievement must first be documented before it can be shared and celebrated.

The Orton Family Foundation has fully embraced the need to qualitatively and quantitatively assess the effects of CM projects on student learning and has begun gathering this data by means of standardized student surveys, pretests, and posttests. These instruments are modified for different age groups, such as elementary, middle, and high school students, and are included in the supplemental CD of CM resources for use by trained CMP staff and educators. Additional qualitative survey instruments have been designed to describe the impacts of CM projects on educators and community partners. It is our hope that the results of properly administered evaluations will be fed into ongoing broad-scale analyses, conducted on behalf of the Foundation by an independent evaluator, and that the collective results will enable us all to broaden the support base for and participation in CM projects.

In terms of community mentors' satisfaction with the CM process and project, if students are not meeting deadlines or producing quality products, mentors can easily burn out and almost certainly lose interest in leading future projects. Appropriate monitoring and final evaluation practices can uncover the need for remedial measures that, if taken, would revitalize the enthusiasm and continued support of project mentors. *Do students have enough class time to work on their tasks? Are community mentors doing more (or less) than they expected to do? Have short-term and long-term project expectations been clearly defined?*

While it is essential for CMP staff to facilitate effective communication among project team members, it can sometimes be difficult to convey apparent shortcomings without the aid of objective assessments. *Is an educator more likely to increase the amount of class time devoted to project work in response to a suggestion by a CMP staff member or a student questionnaire that reveals the same need? What would it take to convince a community mentor that students need more frequent contact and guidance?* Engaging in timely assessments is as important as selecting the appropriate assessment tools and even more critical is the willingness to make the indicated adjustments.

Assessment objective
Plan to assess, document results, and make adjustments as warranted

---

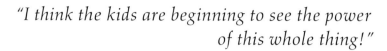

"I think the kids are beginning to see the power of this whole thing!"

**ED HAYNE, SOROCO HIGH SCHOOL SCIENCE TEACHER
OAK CREEK, COLORADO**

Part 4

Training Strategies for Community Mapping Projects

How do you prepare educators—
and ultimately students—for
successful Community Mapping
experiences?

Training strategies

Global positioning systems (GPS) receivers and software are hot items—people are flocking to stores to buy them for all kinds of reasons. We see them being used by hikers and hunters for navigation, by natural resource managers collecting data that will help them delineate habitats, and for organized orienteering games, among many other fun and professional applications. Geographic information systems (GIS) are also growing in popularity along with a demand for training. However, you should keep these points in mind:

- A GIS is only as good as its supporting data.
- GPS units are a good source of data only if used properly.
- There are many other types of data that support GIS.

"Teachers need explicit instruction in how to teach with GIS."

SARAH WITHAM BEDNARZ
IMPACT AND SUCCESS: EVALUATING A GIS TRAINING INSTITUTE

Understanding how GPS and GIS work together, where to find other types of spatial data, and how to integrate all types of nonspatial information into a GIS project—without having to take an advanced, comprehensive course—is only one challenge for CM project teams desiring to learn and apply a new technical tool. This section will examine CM train-the-trainer strategies that require the vigilant merging of four key parts of CM projects: the technical, nontechnical, community, and academic components. It will address the questions: *How do we prepare educators to teach students how to apply GIS to real-world issues and to meet academic standards and goals at the same time?* In other words, *how can educators integrate community-based projects into their curricula and use GIS as a tool to enhance student learning and the understanding of the issues?* And finally, *how can project (community) mentors support this training model?* The process is all about project creation, skills development, and communication.

This section looks at the vertical-slice teaching approach summarized in part 2 at a higher level—one that accommodates the real-world nature of community-based projects and encourages students through each phase of their project with resourcefulness and leadership. Training trainers is certainly a different ball game than teaching end users. We will now consider how this principle plays out in the world of community mapping.

Introducing GIS technology to the trainers

Teaching the mechanics of GIS and GPS technology alone is neither the best way to motivate students, nor to convey to them a sense of the most effective "model of learning." Even giving educators a packed toolbox of lessons and activities has its limitations and drawbacks. *Which lesson do you use first? How much background do students really need?* The CM training model provides an organized approach to training-the-trainers in the context of the interdisciplinary, real-world nature of Community Mapping projects. You may be able to map popular fishing holes in your community . . . *but do you really want to?*

The technological component of CM training typically involves:

- motivated educators
- identification of a community mentor
- brainstorming the issues
- an authentic project
- determining the products needed and what it will take to produce them
- hands-on GIS (computer) work
- working with existing data sets
- field work (GPS, project-specific data collection, such as water quality)
- data assimilation

- engaging appropriate tools at the right time and following a logical process of introducing GIS
- daily evaluations and final workshop evaluations
- producing final GIS layouts and celebrating success

Educators are guided through the steps involved in incorporating GIS into a real community-based project using the same approach that they will want to use with their students. The methodology is transferable between projects and disciplines and the skills taught are basic to most CM projects, for example, the vertical slice approach mentioned in

part 2. Educators are not overwhelmed with more technology than they would reasonably need to initially work with and apply GIS. It is expected that they will gradually build up their skill base over time in concert with the needs of each project, the inspiration and resourcefulness of their students, and the comfort level of the whole project team.

Eight underlying values distinguish The Orton Family Foundation's Community Mapping training from traditional GIS instruction.

The training strategies summarized below reflect the general content, goals, and philosophies of The Orton Family Foundation's CMP workshops. They have been evolving continuously since 1999 and will continue to develop to reflect current knowledge. This manual is not intended to be a substitute for the actual training experience guided by experienced professionals. It is meant to offer insights into a dynamic way of teaching and learning and to support the concept that how trainers are trained can make all the difference.

COMMUNITY MAPPING WORKSHOP	
Approach	**Clarification**
1 Train-the trainer	Teach how to "teach" basic GIS capabilities.
2 Community-based project	Focus on a real community issue with a partner for relevant context.
3 Less is more	Teach one way to accomplish a GIS task versus multiple ways.
4 Need-to-know	Teach GIS skills on a need-to-know basis. What do I really need to know about GIS to tackle this project?
5 Quick to hands-on	Get students in the field and working with GIS as quickly as possible.
6 Roadmap vs. toolbox	Provide teaching aids in an organized, sequential framework to facilitate replication and independent exploration in the classroom and the field.
7 One computer per student	Workshop participants need to do the exercises firsthand in order to retain the skills involved. Assisting neighbors is always encouraged to further reinforce the skills learned and confidence with the technology.
8 Teacher incentives	Graduate and recertification credits, copious food, fun learning environment, data collection field trip, networking breaks, free ArcView site license, and so forth.

Integrating technical and nontechnical applications

The process of integrating a technical tool with nontechnical applications is analogous to teaching someone how to drive a car. Not only do you need to teach the student how to drive the car and provide some basic mechanical and maintenance background, but also the rules of the road, the sociocultural implications. The CM training model explicitly prepares educators and community members to implement GIS and mapping technologies within other existing frameworks, such as curricula and community issues. The key is for educators, in particular, to learn the technology in the same manner as they will teach and lead their students.

Another important consideration in teaching new technical skills to trainers is that they will naturally have different learning styles and comfort levels with the technology. For this reason, CM training allows for these differences by providing an assortment of teaching resources and approaches with a roadmap for their application. Most professional GIS instructors agree that students are capable of running with a new technological tool or concept if they are given the freedom and support to do so. A number of successful CM projects in Colorado were accomplished largely by a few technically-inclined students who mastered GIS beyond the capabilities of their teachers and had the teachers' full support and encouragement. Students who are permitted to troubleshoot

technical problems generally rise to the occasion. Similarly, educators and community mentors can improve their comfort levels by practicing resourceful problem solving when they hit a technical snag in the presence of students.

Effective use of technological tools depends on people. Inherent in the application of GIS to real-world discovery and problem solving is the art of communication—GIS both enhances the understanding and communication of information and depends on communication for relevant depictions of reality. Data and information providers must talk with end users to ensure that the right information is assimilated and what, if any, limitations exist on applying the data.

Critical thinking skills

One measure of how well GIS and mapping skills have been integrated with nontechnical applications, like history or environmental science, is whether students demonstrate critical thinking skills as they carry out their CM project. Critical thinking skills represent a requisite piece of the community mapping process and a valued outcome with respect to student learning. When CM project teams embark on mapping and analyzing various aspects of their community, they need to consider the consequences of publicizing that information, including how the information is organized and presented. Certainly the desires of private citizens to not have personal information freely broadcasted should be respected.

Communication
The bottom line in integrating technical and nontechnical applications

Project teams must communicate about what data they need to gather to address the issue at hand, and how GIS can be used to assimilate and present it in a meaningful way. Would simply mapping where violent crimes have occurred over the past five years provide local officials with sufficient information to justify increasing their police force? Does the data used reflect an accepted definition of "violent" crimes?

Example 1

If it is important to map income distribution or housing costs for development purposes, the data should first be depersonalized, grouped into broad categories and mapped at a larger scale to blur ownership. Creating a community profile of income distribution by age group or by large districts would be a preferable approach.

Example 2

If any features on private property are targeted for mapping, such as historic gravesites, abandoned mines, or nesting sites for an endangered species, permission must first be obtained from the landowners and possibly also from local officials who manage the resource. Students will want to think about who will use the information, for what purposes, and who might be impacted as a result.

Example 3

If students use GPS units to collect original data, such as areas of noxious weed infestations, locations of water quality sampling sites, or state park property lines, they must document their methodology and intended applications. This information is often referred to as metadata. Certainly they have not collected survey-quality location data, but the data may have practical applications if users understand how, why, and when it was gathered. Consulting with appropriate experts before the data is collected can avert liability for data accuracy and misuse.

Involving students in planning discussions regarding data collection and end-use applications necessarily invokes communication and critical thinking skills and requires them to look at situations from multiple angles. Educators and community mentors can play an important role in guiding students to think critically throughout their project and ultimately in using GIS to assist them in decision making. *Now that we know the (relative) location of all the property lines, parking lots, and trails, where (generally) shall park officials install a public restroom? What other considerations need to be taken into account?*

Putting it all together through project management

Organizing the needs, resources, time-lines, goals, technical tools, capabilities and personal interests of educators, community mentors, and students might seem a daunting task. Many dynamic educators and community partners are, in fact, discouraged by the thought of it and avoid CM projects altogether. While CM staff can help with project coordination to a large degree, a project team armed with project management skills operates from a foundation of knowledge, rather than uncertainty, and realistic expectations, instead of idealistic ambitions.

The Orton Family Foundation's Community Mapping Program features a project development and management component, that coupled with the GIS and assessment units, more accurately emulates the flow and sequence of activities in an actual CM project. It is based on a project development flowchart that was developed by a diverse group comprised of CMP staff plus community members and educators with firsthand CM project experience. Project teams needed a framework for developing feasible plans and corresponding responsibilities. They wanted assurance at the outset that what they agreed to do could be accomplished without compromising other commitments.

This flowchart (provided to educators during CM training) is the roadmap for conceiving, designing, and implementing CM projects. It is used and refined at the program level for training the trainers, including new CMP staff, and at the project level for training educators who will be guiding students and often their community partners in CM project work. The process depicted in the flowchart emphasizes anticipating needs, resources and problems through ongoing communication, developing mutual agreements, and constantly assessing progress and adjusting the course as warranted.

Project management skills are vital to affecting a strong partnership between the community mentor and the students—the client–contractor relationship that characterizes CM projects. Project management epitomizes how the real world works. Successful companies have a business plan that they update periodically. Educators follow a course syllabus. The challenge boils down to *how can we effectively combine a business plan with a course syllabus?* This is essentially the task inherent in amalgamating school and community interests with technology thrown in as the magnet.

Project management doctrines compel CM project teams to question various concerns before they become problematic. For example: *Do the students know how to deal with a client—or even adults in general? Does the contractor understand the potential of GIS and how to be a mentor to students? How can educators assure school administrators that the project will indeed help (or has helped) students meet academic standards and may possibly even turn a student around for the better?* What measures of project success and student learning can be built into the project plan at the beginning? A logical approach to addressing these types of concerns is the focus of project management training and the means to a successful and rewarding experience.

Is our project scope small enough yet?

Closing the circle with assessments

Directly aligned with the importance of ongoing communication throughout the CM project is the need for regular student assessments and a final project evaluation. Formative assessments, whatever form they take, must be built into project timelines and curricula to provide constructive feedback and timely encouragement to students during a CM project. They also serve to alert educators and community partners to actual progress or potential problems. Similarly, summative assessments at the end of a CM project are equally important in the quest to continually refine and improve the CM process as a vehicle of service-learning and place-based education.

While most educators are quite skilled at assessing student work, many find that assessing place-based projects or project-based work can be more challenging. This task, in fact, is currently undergoing a major transformation in the place-based education research community in an effort to more quantitatively demonstrate how these types of projects affect student learning and help educators meet academic standards as compared to traditional teaching methods.

The Orton Family Foundation, Vermont Institute of Natural Science, Antioch New England Institute, Shelburne Farms, Wellborn Ecology Fund, and Upper Valley Community Foundataion, and other reputable assessment experts have been collaboratively developing qualitative and quantitative evaluation tools for place-based projects like CM projects. Naturally, the Community Mapping Institute tries to convey the most current and effective assessment philosophies, tools, and approaches available. Grade level pre- and posttests within different disciplines—geography and science, for example—as well as other survey instruments that gauge project effectiveness and outcomes for educators, community partners, and students will be made available to CM Institute participants.

The ultimate success of a CM project, in terms of meeting both academic and community expectations, depends on the how well the project team has integrated technology, education, and real-life processes. The Community Mapping

program accomplishes this by providing train-the-trainer strategies that accommodate these elements in a balanced and logical fashion. GIS for Educators training, for example, introduces educators to the capabilities of GIS and provides a roadmap for teaching others. This training offers a good knowledge base from which to identify a community-based project that would benefit from a GIS or mapping component. Finally, the project management and assessment components bring all the pieces together into a feasible plan-of-action as guided by specific needs and outcomes—effectively building a solid platform for project implementation.

QUESTION #1
How can educators integrate community-based projects into their curricula and use GIS as a tool to enhance student learning?

QUESTION #2
How can we effectively measure the impact of community mapping and other placed-based projects on student learning, educators, and the community?

Adults and youth learning together

Another effective method of introducing GIS to people of all ages is to train them together in a multiday workshop setting; for example, a GIS Day Camp. This represents more of a train-the-first-time-user than a train-the-trainer approach and puts the methodologies taught in the GIS for Educators workshops directly into practice.

A mixed base of participants is a powerful and dynamic combination. It fosters the sharing of a range of perspectives and a range of skills. Often young students are found assisting the adults sitting next to them, which reinforces learning and confidence. It also demonstrates to educators that students can have an impressive, perhaps even latent, capacity for technology that should be encouraged. Educators may grow more comfortable with not having to know more about GIS than their students, because at least one student in each class is likely to be technically adept, venturesome, and eager to provide guidance to their classmates. Notably, a few teachers in Colorado let their students lead the GIS part of their CM projects because they picked up the skills so quickly.

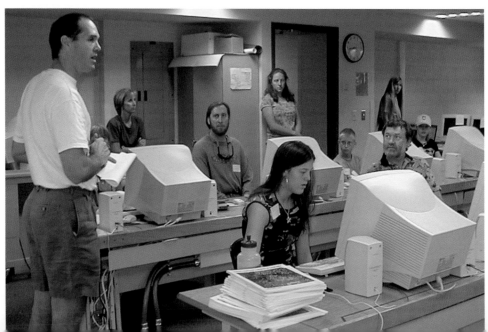

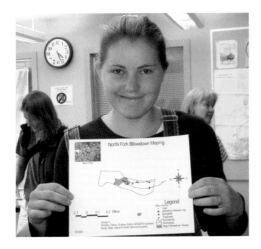

GIS Day Camp: Final maps

The format for training mixed age groups is still based in a real community project since GIS is best learned in the context of relevant applications. GIS Day Camps should provide a combination of hands-on computer lab and fieldwork, and be accessible and inviting to curious parents. The vertical slice of GIS technology covered in a GIS Day Camp—for example, the depth and breadth of topics—may necessarily be narrower than that followed in the Community Mapping Institute, since the knowledge base and learning styles may be more diverse with both students and adults participating. All participants should have created a final GIS product, such as a map or layout, by the end of the Day Camp.

The most rewarding training experiences come from achieving what you set out to do. Clearly communicating and demonstrating desired outcomes at the front end of a workshop establishes a realistic goal and facilitates a sense of accomplishment and closure for each participant.

"Education of place is not about being isolated but about knowing one's self and origin in order to better relate to people in other places."

FROM *LIVING AND LEARNING IN RURAL SCHOOLS AND COMMUNITIES: A REPORT TO THE ANNENBURG RURAL CHALLENGE* (1999)

Part 5

Beyond Community Mapping Projects

This section reflects how a program naturally transforms itself to keep up with the ambitions of its participants. A number of high school students, ranging from the academically motivated to the acutely at-risk, emerged from their Community Mapping projects with a drive to apply their new technical expertise and life skills in ways that have real meaning in the workplace.

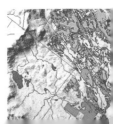

Beyond Community Mapping projects

Everyone has untapped potential that can often be triggered into action by exposure to the right stimulus offered at the right time in the right way. Usually this kind of reaction is connected to a personal passion of some sort, perhaps even a latent interest. *Why is it so important for us to discover and pursue our personal interests and to make a difference? Why do Community Mapping projects seem to hasten the process of self-discovery and self-expression in many young people?* We believe it is related to the direct experience of working in the real world with motivating mentors who effectively engage youth in creative critical-thinking processes. Further, we have seen increased understanding and confidence elicited in students through their use of GIS as a decision-making and graphic communication tool.

When students get excited about a new topic or skill, they deserve opportunities and support to explore their interests more fully—especially as it could relate to jobs and potential career paths. Recognizing the value of extending student-learning experiences beyond CM projects and providing a timely bridge to the professional world, Community Mapping programs can be instrumental in setting up student internships and entry-level jobs with enterprising, reputable community organizations. This section is concerned with the process of developing a framework for effectively introducing motivated students into the local workplace.

"What we see depends mainly on what we look for."

JOHN LUBBOCK

Don't reinvent the framework

Students may see a variety of new interests emerge as a result of their CM project work—including GIS, community planning, journalism, public speaking, and resource management, among others. While it is important to nurture any or all of these special interests, CMP staff will naturally want to focus on implementing internships and jobs that entail the use of GIS or mapping technologies. This may be new territory for established school-to-career programs, but it should attract their attention as a noteworthy opportunity. It is definitely advisable to join forces with a local school-to-career group or school-based vocational counselors to accomplish the following objectives:

1 Co-develop goals and standard criteria (or adopt existing guidelines if available).

2 Pool professional opportunities and student candidates to facilitate the best matches.

3 Enlist experienced help in administering and evaluating the program.

Much like starting a Community Mapping program, the process of conceptualizing and developing an internship program benefits from many perspectives and experiences, especially at the beginning. Forming a coordination committee or advisory group comprised of community members, educators, school-to-career specialists, students, and CMP staff is an excellent way to launch an internship program and to enroll long-term support in the process. A few committee members should represent local businesses and agencies that utilize GIS, because they could speak to the nature and difficulty of the work involved. Community professionals could also offer clear-cut ideas for student projects they would consider hosting and define how the work would address the specific needs of their organizations.

An internship coordination committee will want to answer an initial series of questions, as outlined next, that will guide the conceptualization of a technology-based internship program.

1 Who else should be involved in this committee?

2 What are our internship program goals, scope, and community perspectives?

3 What does a rewarding internship job entail?
- Product vs. no product
- Emphasis on process
- More than data collection and "gofer" tasks
- Constructive feedback throughout
- Responsibility, reliability, and good work ethics

4 What resources exist for matching interested students with host organizations and administering an internship program?

5 What roles should educators, school administrators, school-to-career professionals, and other organizations play in supporting and administering a technology-based internship program?

6 What qualifications or mentoring characteristics should community hosts (or employers) have?

7 Should community hosts be screened prior to implementing an internship? Should their performance be evaluated afterwards?

8 What level of training and skills do students need to qualify for a GIS-based internship?
   - GIS course (through local institutions or CM workshops)
   - Independent study
   - Introductory GIS class at school
   - CM project experience
   - None (will train)
   - Prehire test or skills demonstration
   - Depends on the job
   - GPS proficiency
   - Communication and nontechnical skills

9 What types of compensation will students get (school credit, stipend, salary, benefits) for participating in and successfully completing an internship?

10 Should there be different levels of internships (middle school, high school, community college)? Are there barriers to having middle school students work as interns?

11 How can former interns be encouraged to support new ones?

12 Should students be required to do a final presentation or report when the internship is completed?

13 Who is responsible for providing the necessary equipment (computers, GIS software, GPS units, digital cameras, and so forth)?

14 How might CMP staff support the intern and community host (short- and long-term)?
   - Technical support
   - Web support
   - Provide clearinghouse for internships and job positions
   - Partially fund internships (for example, cost-share based on need)
   - Evaluate and assess the intern's work in collaboration with client and school

15 Who assumes liability for the students' well-being?

16 What does success look like? For the student? For the community host?

Certainly these questions will lead to others, to uncovering the need for additional resources, and to building an effective process that weaves multiple interests and changing perspectives into a program that will ultimately generate rewarding professional experiences for the students and community hosts alike.

Discussions, decisions, designs, and directions make all the difference

Integrating student perspectives into the planning process is essential, especially from students who have worked with GIS and might be interested in an internship themselves. Students with previous internship experiences in any field will also have helpful insights to offer. In a worse-case scenario—the experience is not rewarding—the student and community host or employer might close the door on GIS or internships forever. How these opportunities are set up and who carries them out can make all the difference in individual experiences and also in the sustainability of the program.

In Colorado, the internship coordination committee decided to form a subcommittee that would screen potential partner–student projects. First-time partnerships will naturally require more careful scrutiny and coordination to ensure good matches and positive outcomes. But as the program progresses a database of accumulated experiences could be used to streamline the screening process.

What characteristics of a student candidate and a host partner should the subcommittee evaluate during an initial screening? The Colorado subcommittee came up with the following criteria:

- Willingness of student and community partner to work with an internship screening committee
- Mentoring history or capability of the community partner
- Reliability of the student
- Nature and quality of work (i.e., multifaceted), and degree of GIS proficiency required
- GIS knowledge or technical aptitude of the student
- Feasible timeline
- Flexible schedule (at least during the school year)
- Clear and reasonable expectations
- Fair compensation (pay, stipend, class credit)
- Liability clearly placed with school or employer
- Willingness for assessment and evaluation measures to be built in to determine quality of work, performance, and quality of supervision

The Colorado internship coordination committee also determined that the following three principles were key to designing best-case internship scenarios:

- Developing mentoring relationships
- Building community–school partnerships
- Enabling a symbiotic learning environment for students

"GIS maps are not the most important things for these students to understand—how you get to the map is most important. For example, learning the process of city/county planning versus producing a map."

COLORADO INTERNSHIP COORDINATION COMMITTEE

Concerns were raised that students should not be used as "gofers" for collecting, transcribing, or filing data, but encouraged to further their training and involvement in the broader applications of GIS as a value-added benefit of participating in the program. Additionally, the committee debated whether the GIS-based internship program should be product-driven or process-driven. A product-driven approach, they concluded, would not give students the breadth of understanding that a process-driven approach would.

It is important to also recognize that while a GIS internship may meet all the best-case criteria by giving students a firsthand glimpse into a technology-based career, the experience may actually cause them to realize that GIS is not an overwhelming interest after all. Nevertheless, if the internship was otherwise successful, it would still have been an enlightening, timely, and worthwhile venture for the student.

How much GIS training do students need?

Certainly the base level of GIS expertise could be project-dependent and adapted to the technical proclivity of the student. Some internship programs may elect to set minimum-skills standards for student candidates, such as completing an ArcView class, passing a test administered by the employer–mentor, or demonstrating various skills pertinent to the position. The Colorado coordination committee agreed that a student's degree of interest could be the most important aspect of measuring his or her potential to learn and to succeed. In other words, if the student did not have a burning desire to do that type of work they may not necessarily succeed.

Other internship programs may decide that prospective interns must have completed at least a GIS-based Community Mapping project (for example, they must be able to run a GIS or collect data using GPS units) to qualify. Another exception to the prerequisite GIS class might also apply if an intern participates in a full year or long-term program and the employer is willing to train the intern on the necessary technical skills. After all, don't most mapping projects involve a multifaceted and interactive process of investigation and discovery—and not just the reflexive task of creating a map?

Community Mapping Program role

With the right mix of experts designing and administering the internship program and competent mentors and employers carrying it out, the eventual support role for CMP staff could be minimized to initial matchmaking and screening assistance, periodic interim evaluations, and postinternship evaluations, carried out in accord with the school's review protocol if possible. Most of the CMP's support work would be accomplished prior to a student undertaking an internship, such as through conducting summer training workshops and supporting CM projects during the school year. It would be through their exposure to the CMP's community-based projects,

community mentors, GIS training, and real-world GIS applications that students would be inspired to pursue a related internship. Indeed, several student graduates of CM projects have turned their academic lives around as a result of discovering new interests, technical predispositions, and supportive environments.

A final and very important role that the CMP staff should play is letting community partners know how much their efforts have been appreciated and how they may have made a difference to a young, ambitious self-starter. A close-out celebration or major fuss would definitely make their day!

"I never really noticed how much I cared about the forest and stuff until this year when the project started. I've always wanted to be a scientist and the more times I got out there, it's like, 'oh wow this is really cool. When I grow up, maybe I'll do this'."

EIGHTH GRADE STUDENT DURING A COMMUNITY MAPPING PROJECT IN VERMONT (2002)

Part 6

Community Mapping Project Case Studies

Community Mapping project teams can often tell their own story better than anyone else.

In this section we will introduce you to a number of teams in Vermont and Colorado who have real stories to tell. Stories about place. Not about any place, but about their place—their community. Stories about hard work. Work they did with their communities—rewarding work. Stories about students mastering new skills, learning how the real world works, and using their new knowledge to make a difference in the world in which they live. This is the Community Mapping process at the project level—where the real work happens and service learning begins.

The twelve Community Mapping project case studies summarized here offer a preliminary look at how students, teachers, and community members can work together to learn and apply new skills and accomplish remarkable results given the right opportunity and good support. Collectively, these case study thumbnails reflect copious materials, activities, and final products originated by the twelve project teams, plus the academic curricula, lessons, and assessments used to aid student learning. We hope these brief overviews, covering a range of subjects and issues, will impel new ideas and fuel your confidence to undertake a pilot Community Mapping project in your community.

The Colorado and Vermont project descriptions are organized into three categories as follows:

Ecology and stewardship projects

- Mapping eagle nests
- Beetle infestations
- Carpenter Ranch study
- Wildlife tracking, habitat mapping, landscape conservation/stewardship

Social and economic systems projects

- Historical buildings
- Compass site
- Farm finders express and vital communities demo
- Sharon academy

Transportation and recreation projects

- Rabbit Ears Pass accident mapping
- Steamboat Ski Area trails
- Upper Valley advanced transit system
- Cross-Rivendell Trail project

While methodologies for implementing CM projects may vary, all projects have certain elements in common. These elements provide a practical framework for organizing, presenting, and archiving the various information and tools utilized, especially those that proved most effective. Materials assimilated into a case study portfolio in this way can become a valuable library of resources and ideas that could enhance not only your, but also other's, future CM project experiences. We recommend following the format below (outlined in more detail in part 2) for documenting and presenting a more thorough record of each Community Mapping project. This format allows for telling a story and also for comparing similar characteristics among different projects. Two examples of case study portfolios that were compiled using this format are featured on The Orton Family Foundation's CD of Community Mapping tools, which will be made available to new participating educators and CMP staff.

CASE STUDY TEMPLATE

- Project description
- Background
- Timeline
- Project team member roles
- Project and skills development activities
- Outcomes
- Assessments and evaluations
- Post scripts
- Additional resources

Organizing the project documentation.

Eagle nesting sites: The land of the free and the home of the brave

Lowell Whiteman Primary School students in grades five through eight began a multiyear, eagle nest monitoring project with the Colorado Division of Wildlife (CDOW) to study breeding success rates among bald eagles. Focusing on known nesting sites along the Yampa River in northwest Colorado, students used GPS units to identify their locations. They also recorded additional characteristics of each nest, including height above ground, distance from roadways, and on one occasion,

they were able to work with specialists to record the number of eaglets, nest contents, and other details. The specialists climbed up each tree to examine the nests and using protective bags, carefully lowered any eaglets and nest contents to the ground crew waiting below. While their parents circled above, the eaglets were quickly weighed, measured, photographed, and banded, and then returned to their nests. Although breeding data is important to collect, CDOW wildlife managers were very emphatic about preventing nest disturbance and elected not to visit the nests and band eaglets every year.

The students learned that protecting nesting sites is critical to the long-term well being of the species, as eagles use the same sites over and over, year after year, unless the site is encroached upon or destroyed. Their data analyses may soon begin to show relationships between breeding success, habitat characteristics, and proximity to human disturbances, ultimately leading to recommendations for protecting nesting sites. Mapping locations, recording attributes, and monitoring eagle nesting sites will make it easier to determine whether proposed developments would put a nesting site at risk and may similarly help wildlife managers protect critical eagle habitat. The students will incorporate their findings into an informational document that the CDOW can disseminate to the public.

Elementary students from Steamboat Springs created these GIS maps of eagle nesting sites. The top map shows the nesting sites and various human and natural features of the area. The bottom shows the nesting sites surrounded by concentric rings representing radii in tenth-of-a-mile increments, which makes it easy to determine the proximity of other nearby features.

Beetle infestation: A mighty wind and a mighty bug

Two advanced biology teachers and their students at Steamboat Springs High School adopted a long-term beetle-monitoring project that they helped launch with the U.S. Forest Service during the 2001 GIS Day Camp (a summer workshop for educators and students conducted by the Community Mapping Program in Colorado). As part of their curriculum, the students have collected three years of data already—enough to begin analyzing the potentially epidemic spread of spruce bark beetles within what is known as the "Routt Divide Blowdown." The blowdown occurred in October 1997 when strong winds in excess of 120 miles per hour blew across the Continental Divide, in a path measuring almost five miles wide and thirty miles long, and literally uprooted nearly four million trees on four thousand acres of wilderness within the Routt National Forest.

Unfortunately, large, fallen stands of dead spruce trees are a powerful magnet for spruce bark beetle infestations that are very difficult, if not impossible, to control. Following one treatment method for managing the spread of this very prolific, opportunistic, and destructive beetle, the Forest Service cut down certain areas of infected trees and arranged them into "burn piles" for subsequent controlled burning. Students used GPS units to locate the burn piles and to establish specific study sites on the ground for long-term monitoring of treated and untreated tree infestations. They

are using GIS to map and analyze the infestation data as it changes over time, including the apparent success of treatment measures, with the expectation that this data could someday be used to more accurately forecast beetle infestation behavior. The potential impacts of a beetle epidemic of this nature can be devastating to the ecology, economics, and recreational capacity of an area, especially if a fire were to break out among so much dead timber. This study will keep the students and the Forest Service busy for many years and will ultimately contribute valuable information to the growing base of knowledge on beetle infestations and management.

Students using GPS equipment locate and map a burn pile, where the Forest Service has cut down beetle-infested trees.

In a related project only a few miles from the blowdown area, one of the teachers partnered with the Steamboat Ski and Resort Corporation and engaged nineteen environmental science students in a study of spruce bark beetle and pine beetle infestations within the Steamboat Springs Ski area. Whether these more recent infestations are related to the 1997 blowdown or represent isolated events is not yet known. Students are following a similar investigation as applied in the blowdown study to map, monitor, and analyze the rates and direction of spruce and pine beetle infestations among trees stands on the ski mountain. The more the dynamics of invasive beetle infestations are understood, the more prepared residents, resource managers, and businesses will be to work together to control and prevent devastating outbreaks. While effective solutions to the multifaceted beetle infestation problems in the Steamboat area remain unproven, students are hopeful that their long-term monitoring efforts and the Forest Service's controlled testing of various treatments will soon lead to badly needed answers.

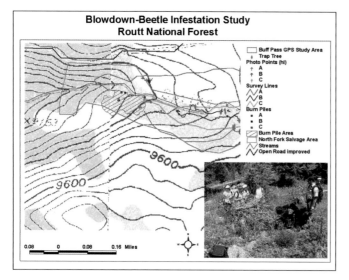

Carpenter Ranch land management

The Hayden High School Environmental Science Club teamed up with The Nature Conservancy on a three-part project to study the Carpenter Ranch land along the Yampa River in northwest Colorado. Phase one called for students to use GPS units to locate twelve or thirteen existing groundwater wells for future monitoring studies. Considerable time was spent actually finding the well sites, as the original researcher, a graduate student, did not mark them. The results will enhance the understanding of how vegetation patterns follow groundwater and river levels. It will help fill in the ecological model of riparian systems along the Morgan Bottoms Reach of the Yampa River and tie in with ditch consolidation work. Ultimately, the information these students collect will help The Nature Conservancy and nearby landowners make wiser land- and water-management decisions.

Phase two of the Carpenter Ranch project focused on fish habitat and slough mapping and was conducted by a Hayden High School science class. Using GPS units and ArcView, students mapped sloughs, beaver dams, and other natural and man-made features along the river that might provide or affect fish habitat. With the help of students of all ages in the Hayden School District, The Nature Conservancy maintains a growing database of information about the Carpenter Ranch property. A portion of that database is now archived in ArcView

as a result of the students' work and aids in the ongoing conservation and management efforts on the ranch.

In phase three, Hayden Middle School students mapped Yampa River cross-sections in stable and unstable reaches and tied the results to historic hydrologic events. This information will provide insights to The Nature Conservancy on riverbank management strategies.

A team in the field, locating and mapping a well with a GPS unit.

The 2002 Slough Study.

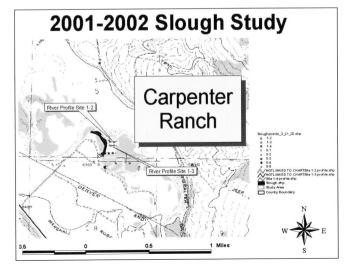

Tracking in Vermont

The Program of Audubon Research for Teens, sponsored by Vermont Audubon, sent a team of high-school-aged campers into Vermont's West Mountain Wildlife Management Area and the Silvio O. Conte National Wildlife Refuge, two former commercial logging areas that had recently entered public ownership. The team gathered information about the presence of animal species and use of habitat that will be used and may be critical to land-use planning, management, and conservation of wildlife habitats. Using GPS units, students looked for and geolocated animal tracks, feeding signs, scat, and other markings, finding evidence after four days in the field of turkey, mink, moose, black bear, river otter, beaver, ermine, coyote, bobcat, red fox, and porcupine.

Students working in Vermont's Phenn Basin used GPS equipment to geolocate evidence of wildlife in a former logging area, and created this map using aerial photography, topographic data, and the field data they collected. Both the Take PART and Harwood projects were led by Sean Lawson of Keeping Track (c), as part of that conservation organization's program to introduce young people (K-12) to wildlife habitat monitoring and to instill an appreciation for healthy natural areas, via teaching tools such as GIS and GPS, methods, and skills in wildlife tracking, biology, and habitat conservation.

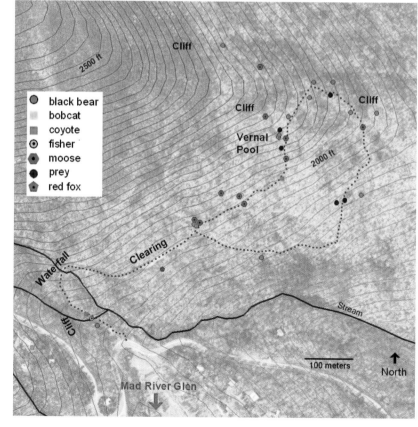

Historical buildings: The past can be mapped, too

A freshmen class of about forty students identified and used GPS units to geolocate historic buildings in South Routt County, Colorado, and then researched the origins, history, and relocations of each building. Following the Historic Walking Tour project model developed for Steamboat Springs the previous year, students wrote enlightening histories, gathered old pictures, took new digital photos of each historic building, and then used GIS to archive and display their accumulated information. During a conference presentation about their project, a few freshman girls demonstrated how to "hotlink" a building photo to a location on the ArcView map, showing all the steps and involving the audience. Photos and descriptive text were hotlinked to their respective GIS site locations, allowing anyone to easily access the data without having to handle any fragile photos and documents.

The freshman class continued this project during their sophomore year, effectively reinforcing their GIS, critical thinking, and public speaking skills, while also adding to the base of historical information maintained by the Routt County Historic Preservation Society. The students' work will provide timely input to a visitor's brochure and the museum's Web site, as well as graphic input for grant proposals and applications to the National Register of Historic Buildings. This Community Mapping project has definitely increased the sense of place for many students and adults in South Routt County.

The Antlers Café and Bar, and the Yampa Bible College, two historic buildings in South Routt County. Student work in identifying and cataloging these and other sites will be used in a number of different ways as part of general community educational outreach by three community partners: Routt County Historic Preservation Society, Phippsburg–Oak Creek Historical Society, and the Tread of Pioneers Museum.

Students presenting a hotlink demonstration at a conference.

The Compass site: GIS and a hand-painted town mural

Meanwhile, another group of seventh- and eighth-graders, from the Compass School of Westminster Station, Vermont, conducted a similar investigation of the history and critical systems of a nearby mill town, Bellows Falls. Once one of the most prosperous towns in the nation, the fortunes of Bellows Falls declined, like many other mill towns.

Working from a historical Beers (a post-Civil War company of surveyors) Atlas of the town, students created a wall-sized mural of the town, georeferencing points of interest and importance with GIS, then incorporating the styles of various Vermont artists to create a truly original and unique portrait of a town. Field work in this project involved a technique known as "Parish Mapping," which calls for direct contact between mappers and the area they wish to map: boundaries are established, and the neighborhood or village is scouted on foot. By interviewing residents, personal histories, anecdotes, rituals, and other aspects of the social continuity of a place become an essential part of the map.

The Bellows Falls Mural (left)combines sophisticated GIS technology, which allowed precise location of historical points, and old-fashioned hand-crafting. The result is a beautiful, graphically rich, and annotated Parish Mapping portrait. An orthophoto of Bellows Falls (shown on the right) offers a very different view of the area.

Farm Finders Express

As part of a program at the Richards
Free Library in Newport, New Hampshire, home-schooled children ranging
in age from eight to fourteen inter-
viewed vendors at the Newport Farmers'
Market, then visited the actual farms.
The goal of the project was to support
and promote the consumption of local farm products. Using GIS; digital
topographic maps; orthophotos; descriptions of the farms, the farmers, and their
products; and contact information, a
Web site was created that has helped the
Newport Market grow to be the second-
largest such market in the state.

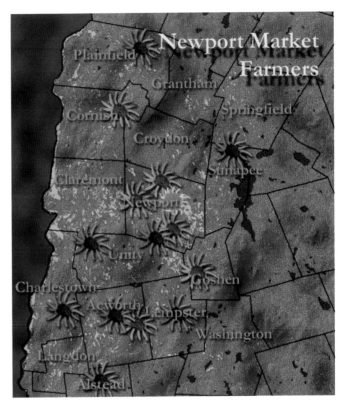

This map, created by home-schoolers aged eight to fourteen, can be found
on the World Wide Web at Farm Finders Express. Clicking on a flower icon
brings up detailed information gathered by the students about a particular
participating farm.

Town planning: Mapping a vision of Sharon

The town of Sharon is creating a vision plan for the next fifty years. They are creating development guidelines with the input of town residents to help retain the essence of their small town as the future brings continued growth and urban sprawl to northern New England. Seventh and eighth grade students at Sharon Academy, with the help of town planners, have generated a survey that went out to every household in the town, to be voluntarily completed and returned. The results will be compiled into a short document expressing the essence of the town of Sharon. Students have used the results of the surveys to map the special places that residents described. Students are also creating GIS maps of the town highlighting natural resources and development trends.

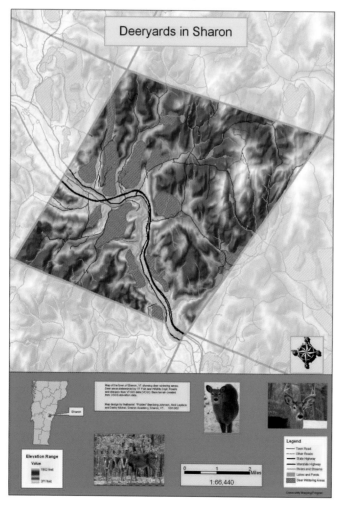

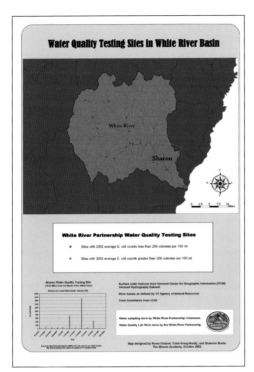

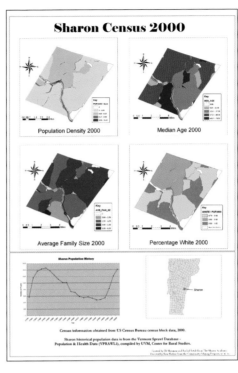

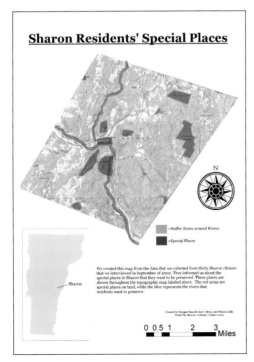

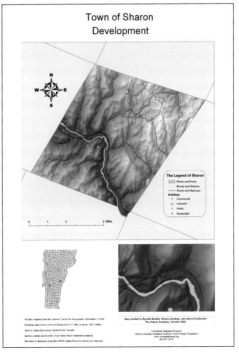

Rabbit Ears Pass: Accident mapping before and after skiing

This study focused on a very busy mountain pass that provides access to and from a ski resort town, Steamboat Springs. Students acquired ten years of recorded accident data from the Colorado Department of Transportation and quickly realized that they would have trouble mapping accident locations in a GIS. This is because the accidents were recorded relative to mile markers along the highway, for example, "about halfway between mile markers 139 and 140" or "a quarter mile east of mile marker 148." In order to more precisely map the locations of the accidents, the students decided to use GPS units to accurately locate mile marker positions and then extrapolate accident locations from these known points. At each mile marker, they also took digital photos in both directions to capture the general layout and terrain of the highway and hotlinked the photos to their respective mile marker points in the GIS. They presented their initial results to the Steamboat Springs Ambulance Service and Routt County Commissioners and were earnestly encouraged to use GIS to tackle more specific analyses during the next school year that would shed further light on possible causes and remedies in high-incident areas.

Students using GPS units to map mile markers along Rabbit Ears Pass, a heavily used stretch of highway leading into and out of a destination ski resort. As a result of the students' recommendations, the Steamboat Springs Ambulance Service has begun equipping their emergency response vehicles with GPS units.

Working closely with the Steamboat Springs Ambulance Service during the second year, students added more accident data to their GIS and began analyzing trends and suggesting ways to reduce accidents. They considered many variables, including driver age, gender, vehicle type, time of day, road conditions, weather, season, and other information, and came up with some very enlightening results and initial recommendations. Their next steps will involve analyzing the costs associated with responding to accidents and the potential savings that could be realized through various mitigation measures, from signage and reduced speed limits to highway improvements. The Ambulance Service credits the students for not only contributing to the county's highway safety plan, but also for providing strong justification that ambulances be equipped with GPS units and other technology that will enable their crews to record accurate accident data more efficiently while they are on a call.

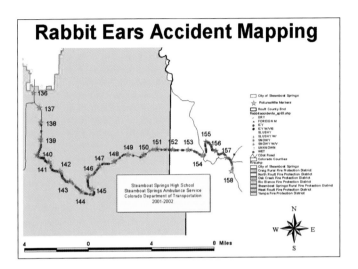

One of many ArcView layouts the students created showing various relationships between accident locations and other variables, such as weather-related road conditions, on Rabbit Ears Pass. Students were able to identify accident hot spots by comparing numbers of accidents that have occurred between mile markers, represented by red stars.

Steamboat Springs High School students presenting the results of their analyses of accident trends on Rabbit Ears Pass to the Routt County Emergency Management Service Advisory Council.

The business of skiing: Steamboat Ski Area trails

Two groups of students, one from Steamboat Springs High School and one from nearby Lowell Whiteman High School, worked independently with Steamboat Ski and Resort Corporation to begin the process of building a base map of the corporation's ski area.

The Whiteman group used GPS units and GIS to map ski trail boundaries, tree pods, and ski trail intersections on the mountain. The project fit easily into both the students' GIS class and elective ski-training program. The students eventually want to help Steamboat Ski Corp. analyze how grooming patterns, snow depth, and snowfall volume might affect the cost of grooming and snowmaking operations. The Ski Corp. spends many

staff and equipment hours on grooming operations. Current operations are less efficient than they could be because it is difficult for the equipment operators to determine snow depth along the trails. Hence, this Community Mapping project represents the first phase of a long-term effort that will eventually equip snow cats with ground-sensing radar capable of displaying real-time snow depth for trail groomers as they move around the mountain maintaining ski trails. The new data and equipment will allow them to move deeper snow to shallow areas much more efficiently than in the past. The net cost savings to the Steamboat Ski Corp. to make and groom snow on Mount Werner's ski trails will also be tremendous.

The Steamboat Springs group used GPS equipment to locate the positions of snow-making hydrants on the lower ski mountain. The Steamboat Ski Corp. spends enormous amounts of money each year making snow, particularly in the early part of the ski season when safe skiing conditions may not otherwise exist. When snowmaking hydrants cannot be found and turned on in a timely manner, time and money are wasted, critical areas of the mountain may not reach desired snow depths, and additional expense can be incurred as grooming teams are mobilized to move snow into problem areas. The Ski Corp. also requested that the students take photographs and record specific attributes about each hydrant,

Students worked the slopes outside, on skis, with GPS equipment, and inside, on computers loaded with GIS.

including the model type and identification number, whether it had handles and air locks, the composition and condition of the lid if present, and whether it was underground or above ground. Students downloaded their data into a GIS and hotlinked photos of each hydrant to their respective sites. In subsequent phases of this project, the students will use the data to help the Ski Corp. analyze water use and associated costs of snowmaking.

Prior to these two Community Mapping projects, the Steamboat Ski Corp. did not use GPS and GIS technologies to manage slope maintenance operations. Accurate locations and maps of ski trails and snowmaking hydrants will now help to make snowmaking and trail grooming more cost-efficient endeavors for slope managers at this ski area.

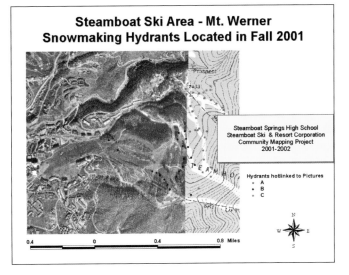

Steamboat Ski Area Trail Boundaries

Yoohoo.shp
Voguepolyline1.shp
Vagabpoly2.shp
Topofgondypolygood.shp
Tompoly2.shp
Southfacepark.shp
Smvtrk3poly.shp
Shortcutpoly.shp
Seempolywhole.shp
Rudis.shp
Rightowaypoly.shp
Littlebasepolygon.shp
Heavenlydaze.shp
Goodbashor.shp
Gigglegulch.shp
Betwix.shp
Betweenpoly.shp
Basepolygon.shp

Steamboat Ski Area - Mt. Werner Snowmaking Hydrants Located in Fall 2001

Steamboat Springs High School
Steamboat Ski & Resort Corporation
Community Mapping Project
2001-2002

Hydrants hotlinked to Pictures
A
B
C

Upper Valley advanced transit system: Get on the bus!

The Upper Valley Transportation Management Association runs a fleet of free buses in Hanover and Lebanon, Vermont. Funded by the Dartmouth Hitchcock Medical Center, Dartmouth College, and the state, it's a part of what statistics indicate will soon be the largest and busiest public transportation system in the state. The buses are clean and comfortable and run on time. And yet ridership, until recently, was not at the level proponents hoped it would be.

Nine high school students from around the country—including two from the local area—and two CM educators came together to assess the problem as part of a CMP Summer Institute seminar held at Colby-Sawyer College in New London, New Hampshire. They were joined by a community partner (Steve Glazer of Vital Communities) and a seminar lecturer (Denis Wood, author of *Power of Maps* and *Seeing Through Maps: The Power of Images to Shape*

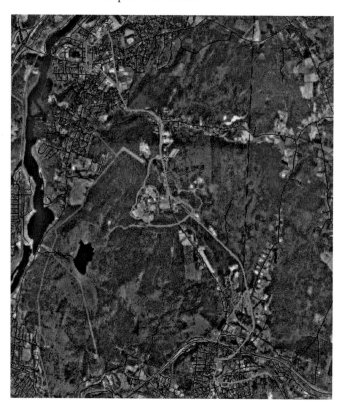

Our World View). They identified four goals: increased ridership, improved maps, leveraged resources, and clearer articulation to the community of the benefits of public transportation.

The group split into four teams: one to ride the bus, interview other riders and drivers, and take digital video footage; and three to find, document (with photographs and data sheets), and map (with GPS receivers) bus stops along the Blue Route, a major transportation corridor connecting the biggest of the area's employers and the usual assortment of amenities.

When the group reconvened after a day of fieldwork, their findings were conclusive: it wasn't easy to find the stops. (Even the group that rode the buses agreed.) The scale of the map currently in use lacked significant reference features and was on a scale that allowed for little detail. The rest of the seminar was devoted to analysis and the making of new, better maps.

A great deal was learned in a very short period of time about the complicated nature of public transportation. As one participant put it: "I learned that removing cost as a barrier is, in and of itself, insufficient to move significant numbers of people out of their cars." This is a sobering but important observation to keep in mind as the country learns about and adapts to new ways of keeping itself moving.

Connecting communities in Vermont and New Hampshire: The Cross Rivendell Trail project

As the only K-12 interstate school district in the nation, Rivendell has an ambitious mission of community-based education at its core. The Cross Rivendell Trail now unites the towns of Orford, New Hampshire; Fairlee, West Fairlee, and Vershire, Vermont, and has the potential to be a powerful educational tool that

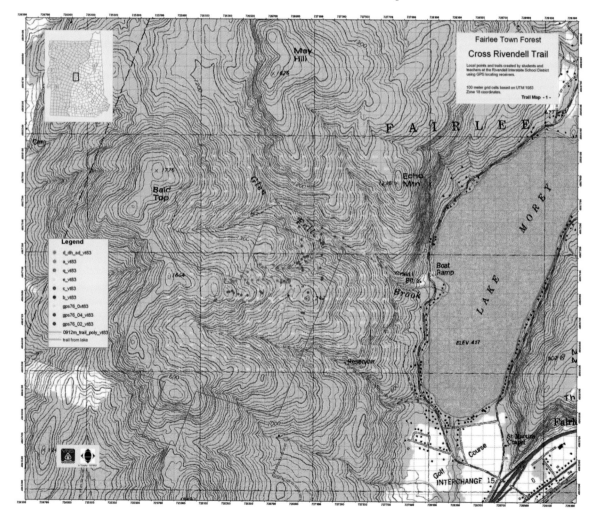

Fairlee Town Forest

Cross Rivendell Trail

Local points and trails created by students and teachers at the Rivendell Interstate School District using GPS locating receivers.

100 meter grid cells based on UTM 1983 Zone 18 coordinates.

Trail Map - 1 -

Legend
- d_dh_ad_vt83
- a_vt83
- q_vt83
- e_vt83
- c_vt83
- b_vt83
- gps78_0vt83
- gps76_04_vt83
- gps76_02_vt83
- 0912m_trail_poly_vt83
- trail from lake

honors the integrity of traditional Upper Valley culture, advances the learning of students, and brings together sometimes conflicting interests in the community.

A CM project contributed to the design and development of the trail. Using a series of orthophotos with Universal Transverse Mercator grids superimposed on them, the students worked out and suggested prospective trail routes. Fieldwork with GPS receivers allowed them to geolocate potential trail features and constraints—the good and the bad, in other words, of each possible trail as

The Rivendell area as a topographic map, and as an orthophoto overlaid with GPS-collected trail points, features, and commentary.

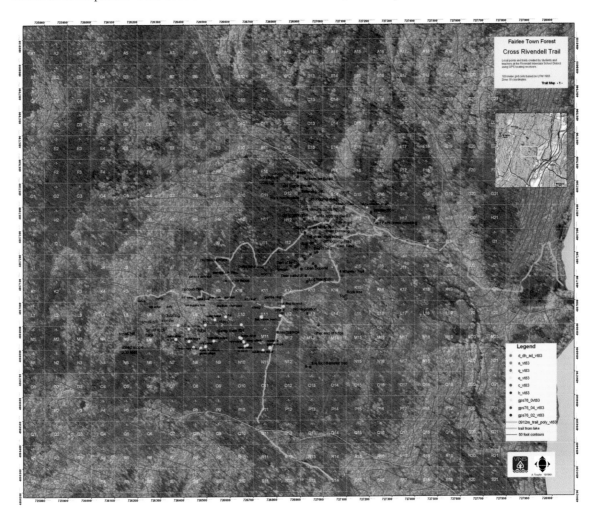

Two Rivendell students mark a tree along a stretch of prospective trail. Community Mapping projects combine complex technologies, like GIS and GPS, and the blood, sweat, and tears of field work.

Presentation of findings and recommendations is the important final step in a CM project.

it existed in the real world. When the trail design was completed, the students used the wall maps of the orthophotos and topographic maps as part of a collage (with photos and findings) to present their ideas and work to a district wide meeting. This transportation and trail design project did a nice job of integrating field work and spatial data to address a community need.

The project was part of a course for eleventh and twelfth graders that was designed and developed to examine human interaction with natural systems from social, economic, and environmental (physical) perspectives, in topics ranging from biodiversity and species extinction to consumerism and "the American Dream." The course mixed readings, journaling, lab work, and discussion, with the trail project, and a second long-term project: analysis of the academy's "ecological footprint." Throughout the course students wrestled with these two real-life case studies as a context for investigating the causes and consequences of human activity.

"Knowledge carries with it the responsibility to see that it is well used in the world."

DAVID W. ORR
EARTH IN MIND: ON EDUCATION, ENVIRONMENT, AND THE HUMAN PROSPECT

Part 7

Additional Resources

While the focus and concerns of CM projects are emphatically local and immediate, resources can be found around the world. Here are links, ideas, and bridges for further inquiry and research.

As Dr. Joseph J. Kerski aptly pointed out in his foreword, Community Mapping projects "are engaging because they involve rapidly changing, exciting, spatial technologies that are quickly becoming part of everyday life." More and more sources of spatial data, mapping tools, and innovative online mapping resources are materializing every day as these technologies facilitate an ever-expanding array of human tasks—from the simplest to the most complex applications. As this book goes to print, GIS is being used to track the myriad fallen remains of the space shuttle Columbia, following its tragic disintegration upon reentry into our atmosphere on February 1st, 2003. In this case, GIS will help scientists determine how and why Columbia met its catastrophic fate, in the hope that such occurrences may be prevented in future space flights.

While it can be said that the Community Mapping Program relies primarily on people, interactions, and relationships, spatial technologies must be recognized for the power they have to spark initial interest and then propel community–school projects into life. We would be remiss if we did not acknowledge the vast and growing pool of spatial resources available to us all. The breadth and depth of readily accessible tools and data testifies to the magnitude of interest in the geospatial field, as well as our mounting dependence on its capacity to help us understand our world and manage its resources. Kids have not been overlooked in the least—many online spatial resources are emerging that are specifically designed to engage young students in the magic and power of GIS early on.

This section attempts to capture a representative sample of the accessible mapping resources we currently have at our fingertips. Do not forget to check your local community to acquire equally valuable data for your own CM projects. We know this list is not exhaustive (The Orton Family Foundation's Community Mapping Web site, *www.communitymap.org*, maintains a more extensive and current list), and will quickly be outdated, given lifespans on the Web. We hope, nevertheless, that it will inspire you and your students to surf the Internet regularly to discover the latest additions and improvements and innovations. You may find yourself contributing some of your own!

Table of contents

Web resources: GIS and mapping

Colorado
csf.colorado.edu/bcw/index.html
The Boulder Creek Watershed site is hosted by Communications for a Sustainable Future, sponsored by The Naropa Institute and the Boulder Creek Watershed Initiative Site.

Earth Island Institute
www.earthisland.org/borneo/ourwork/mapping.html
Earth Island Institute: Borneo Project. Community-based mapping of traditional village land in the rainforest of Sarawak, East Malaysia.

ESRI
www.esri.com
The Environmental Systems Research Institute, Inc. (ESRI) Web site has extensive information on GIS software, data, and resources.

Geography Network℠
www.geographynetwork.com
Geography Network: A comprehensive source for online GIS maps, data, and services.

Green Map
www.greenmap.com
The Green Map System is a globally connected, locally adaptable ecocultural program for community sustainability.

Indonesia
www2.eastwestcenter.org/environment/fox/kali.html
Mapping Customary Land in East Kalimantan, Indonesia: A research paper on using mapping in order to delineate the customary land rights of indigenous communities.

Land Trust Alliance
landtrustalliance.bc.ca/public
Watch the Land Trust Alliance of British Columbia for continuing work with artists and communities to explore the human–ecological dimensions of the Salish Sea.

Maya Mapping Project

geography.berkeley.edu/ProjectsResources/MayanAtlas/MayaAtlas/MayanAtlas2.html

The Mayan Atlas showcases the Maya Mapping Project to protect the homeland of the Toledo Maya of southern Belize.

National Aeronautics and Space Administration

www.nasa.gov

National Geographic Society

www.nationalgeographic.com

National Oceanic and Atmospheric Administration

www.noaa.gov

National Oceanic and Atmospheric Administration: Current U.S. satellite images, radar images, and animated maps.

United States Geological Survey

www.usgs.gov
mapping.usgs.gov/digitalbackyard
Explanation of the creation of USGS's most widely used digital maps.
ask.usgs.gov
Earth Science Information Center

Washington

www.fish.washington.edu/naturemapping/index.html
Nature Mapping is a program focused in Washington State with the goal of making communities and individuals aware of their natural resources and offering tools to monitor these resources. Check out their workshops and maps of the predicted distributions of various species.

Web resources: GIS and education

Center for Environmental Education
www.schoolsgogreen.com
Center for Environmental Education of Antioch New England Institute: Site contains tools and information about integrating environmental education into all aspects of the K-12 experience.

Center for Highly Interactive Computing in Education
hi-ce.org
Center for Highly Interactive Computing in Education: Investigation Station. Source of Tech Ed software, including Model-It. Resources and software for students and teachers.

Center for Image Processing
www.cipe.com
Center for Image Processing in Education (CIPE): A not-for-profit organization that promotes computer-aided visualization as a tool for teaching and learning. CIPE conducts workshops and develops instructional materials that use image processing and GIS technologies as platforms for teaching about science, mathematics, and technology.

Colorado
www.colorado.edu/geography/gcraft/contents.html
The Geographer's Craft: The University of Colorado at Boulder hosts a very useful series of lecture notes (*www.Colorado.EDU/geography/gcraft/notes/notes.html*)on topics such as coordinate systems, data sources, accuracy, and GIS.
www.cde.state.co.us/index_stnd.htm
Colorado Model Content Standards: Standards and expectations organized by subject, such as geography and science.

Concord Consortium
www.concord.org
The Concord Consortium is dedicated to furthering the teaching and learning revolution worldwide through innovations in hardware, software, learning environments, curricula, and institutions.
csf.concord.org
Center for a Sustainable Future, a division of the Concord Consortium.

Edgewood Watershed Education Connection

natsci.edgewood.edu/watershed

The Edgewood Watershed Education Connection: Contains resources for teachers on topics including watersheds, mapping, and ecosystem health. The mapping information (*danenet.wicip.org/gisedu/homepage/maps/Default.htm*)is useful for explaining general mapping, GIS, and ArcView.

Educational Standards

edStandards.org/Standards.html

Putnam Valley Schools, New York: A comprehensive repository for online sources on standards (organized by subject, state, and so forth).

Eisenhower National Clearinghouse

www.enc.org

Eisenhower National Clearinghouse for Science and Mathematics Education provides an extensive listing of curriculum resources, professional resources, and Web links for teachers.

Enviroarts

arts.envirolink.org

EnviroArts: The Arts and Education section has teacher reflections on placed-based learning and cultivating an understanding of the natural world.

ESRI

www.esri.com/data/online/ArcData

Community Atlas: Teachers and students work to develop descriptions and maps of their community. The resulting projects (*gis.esri.com/industries/k-12/commatlas/browse.cfm*) can be searched and viewed through this Web site. Completion of the final project earns the participating K-12 school rewards (*www.esri.com/industries/k-12/atlas/details.html#reward*) such as ArcView software or extensions, along with a site license.

www.esri.com/industries/k-12

GIS for Schools and Libraries. Information about using GIS in K-12 schools, public or college libraries, museums, nature centers, and other sites for educating the public.

www.esricanada.com/english/education/resources.asp#EducationResources

Includes literature and papers including "GIS in School Curricula" and "Techniques for Using GIS in the Classroom."

Florida

nersp.nerdc.ufl.edu/%7Erol1851/community/maps_project.html
The Community Maps Project is a joint project between University of Florida art students and local elementary school children to create community maps.

GLOBE

www.globe.gov
GLOBE (Global Learning and Observations to Benefit the Environment) is a worldwide program for students to take scientific measurements, input data over the Web, and create maps online to analyze data.

Kansas

kangis.org
KanGIS is KanCRN's K-12 GIS community, resourcing the Kansas Collaborative Research Network site with informative papers concerning GIS in the classroom. You can also navigate through the remainder of the site to learn more about KanCRN data, maps, and lessons.

Maine

www.state.me.us/education/lres/lres.htm
State of Maine's Learning Results document.

National Aeronautics and Space Administration

education.nasa.gov
NASA Education Program
kids.msfc.nasa.gov
NASA Kids provides hundreds of Web pages about space science, rockets and airplanes, and pioneers and astronauts. Teachers can find puzzles, games, and coloring pages, and (in the Teacher's Corner) can subscribe to a newsletter. (NASA)
esdcd.gsfc.nasa.gov/ESD/edu
NASA's Earth Science Educator provides 160 links to student projects, teacher resources, software, data sets, and more, with appropriate grade levels marked. The topics cover the deep earth, the ground, the atmosphere, and space.
spacelink.nasa.gov/Instructional.Materials/Curriculum.Support/Earth.Science/Geography
Spacelink-Geography: Numerous links to background and educational materials on mapping.
wwwedu.ssc.nasa.gov/ltp
NASA's From A Distance: Lesson plans are available for giving students an introduction to remote sensing, GPS, and GIS.

National Center for Geographic Information and Analysis

www.ncgia.ucsb.edu/education/ed.html

National Center for Geographic Information and Analysis (NCGIA): Site includes information on the NCGIA Education Program *(www.ncgia.ucsb.edu/education/ed.html)* as well as their Core Curriculum for GIS Science *(www.ncgia.ucsb.edu/giscc)*.

National Geographic Society

www.nationalgeographic.com/education

Education categories include online adventures, maps and geography lesson plans, teacher's community, and teacher's store. This site is rich in special resources and activity sections for kids, parents, students, and teachers.

National Geography Standards

www.nationalgeographic.com/resources/ngo/education/standards.html

"Geography for Life" National Geography Standards. National Geographic site that links to a list of the eighteen National Geography Standards and gives order information for the entire 272-page document.

New Hampshire

www.ed.state.nh.us/CurriculumFrameworks/curricul.htm

New Hampshire Curriculum Frameworks

North Carolina

www2.ncsu.edu/ncsu/cep/ligon/about/history/esri/P7311.htm

Ligon History Project: Exploring the Past to Influence the Future is a collaborative project between middle school students, teachers, alumni, and university professors and students to document the history of Ligon High School in Raleigh, North Carolina.

www.ncsu.edu/midlink/gis/gis_intro.htm

GIS/GPS Technology at Ligon. The Ligon GT Magnet Middle School Web site provides an outline of their GIS course, student projects, and GIS Web links.

Orion Society

www.orionsociety.org

Orion Society: An environmental education organization, and a communications and support network for grassroots environmental and community organizations across North America.

The Orton Family Foundation

www.communitymap.org

The Orton Family Foundation's Community Mapping Program Web site: a collection of resources and opportunities pertaining to the design, implementation, and delivery of CM projects. Training events, student products, and project descriptions (Map Gallery), and other online resources are organized for easy access by educators, students, and community members.

www.orton.org

The Orton Family Foundation's main Web site describes various Foundation products and programs, including CommunityViz, Community Video, the book *Hands on the Land*, and Community Mapping.

Rocky Mountain Mapping Center

rockyweb.cr.usgs.gov/public/outreach

USGS–Rocky Mountain Mapping Center's education and outreach site. Click on their "GIS in Education" link.

Rubistar

rubistar.4teachers.org

RubiStar: Create Rubrics for your Project-Based-Learning Activities. RubiStar is a tool to help the teacher who wants to use rubrics but does not have the time to develop them from scratch.

Rural School and Community Trust

www.ruraledu.org

Rural School and Community Trust: Connecting rural schools with their communities in order to foster rural life and place-based learning.

State Education and Environmental Roundtable

www.seer.org

State Education and Environment Roundtable (SEER): SEER developed Environment as an Integrating Context (EIC)—an educational approach involving the use of the school's surroundings and community as a framework for learning. From this site you can view an executive summary of their report Closing the Achievement Gap: Using the Environment as an Integrating Context for Learning (*www.seer.org/pages/GAP.html*). Education for sustainability and other education connections.

United States Geological Survey
geology.er.usgs.gov/eastern/inquiries.html
USGS Education and Outreach provides links to geologic information for the public, educators, students, scientists, and businesses. The principal areas are the environment, geologic hazards (such as earthquakes and volcanoes), minerals and fossils, geologic maps, and more. (USGS)
mapping.usgs.gov/www/html/1educate.html
USGS's Educational Resources for Cartography, Geography, and Related Disciplines offers fact sheets and booklets on various geological topics and links to the Learning Web of the U.S. Geological Survey, the National Atlas of the United States, satellite images, and educational packets.
www.usgs.gov/education
Learning Web resources for students (homework help and project ideas), teachers (lesson plans, activities, paper models, and animation), and research tools for anyone interested in natural science.
water.usgs.gov/public/education.html
USGS Water Resources Education Resources is a collection of fun classroom activities that teach students about various aspects of water. There is an interactive center where students can give opinions and test their water knowledge, "FrogWeb" which focuses on amphibian declines and deformities, free education posters on wetlands and water use, and more.

Vermont
www.state.vt.us/educ
State of Vermont Department of Education: Information clearinghouse with useful Vermont links.
www.vinsweb.org
Vermont Institute of Natural Science (VINS): Protecting Vermont's natural heritage through education and research designed to engage individuals and communities in the active care of their environment. VINS actively disseminates the Community Mapping Program through a partnership with The Orton Family Foundation.
geology.uvm.edu/landscape/highschools.html
Landscape Change Project: Vermont K-16 students are contributing to an online archive of historical and modern photos of the Vermont landscape in order to document change.

Woodrow Wilson Foundation

www.woodrow.org/teachers/esi/1997/02/CORE.htm

Land Use and Land Cover: Using Geographic Information Systems to develop a Sense of Place. A project of the Environmental Science Core Institute, Woodrow Wilson National Fellowship Foundation.

Worldwatcher

www.worldwatcher.nwu.edu

WorldWatcher software for visually analyzing scientific data can be downloaded from this site. The site also discusses its middle school and high school curriculum initiative.

Web resources: Data

BASINS

www.epa.gov/ostwater/BASINS

BASINS: EPA's Better Assessment Science Integrating Point and Nonpoint Sources (BASINS) integrates GIS, watershed and meteorologic data, and modeling tools into one convenient package. "It's a rich Web site with data about watersheds in the forty-eight conterminous states that can be used for detailed GIS projects. It's even a bit intimidating. BASINS was designed for people doing hardcore watershed analysis, and they have created sophisticated applications using ArcView which can be downloaded or ordered for free." —Charlie Fitzpatrick, ESRI Schools and Libraries. Detailed instructions for using BASINS from ESRI are located at *www.esri.com/industries/k-12/basins.html*

Berkeley Digital Library

sunsite.berkeley.edu/GIS/gisnet.html

Berkeley Digital Library's Guide to GIS Resources on the Internet. Contains a comprehensive listing of GIS Web resources, and great links to federal and state data sources.

Colorado

www.dola.state.co.us/oem/cartography/cartog.htm

Colorado Cartography and Mapping: Colorado GIS data (including boundaries, school districts, census data) is available for downloading . You can also download PDF or JPEG versions of Colorado maps.

ESRI

www.esri.com/data/download/census2000_tigerline

Census TIGER® Data: Download local census geospatial data aggregated by either census block or census tract.

Fish and Wildlife Service

www.fws.gov/data/gishome.html

U.S. Fish and Wildlife Service, GIS and Spatial Data site provides links to GIS data by state, as well as to agency and national data sets.

Geography Network

www.geographynetwork.com

Geography Network: Categories include free data resources, live data services, and clearinghouses. Data is available from sources such as ESRI, National Atlas, and National Wetlands Inventory.

GIS Data Report

data.geocomm.com

GIS Data Depot has digital data on the state or county wide level available for free download.

Landsat

www.landsat.org

Search for Landsat 7 satellite images.

MAGIC Map and Geographic Information Center

magic.lib.uconn.edu

MAGIC Map and Geographic Information Center: A University of Connecticut site that has Connecticut, New England, and United States data. This site also contains general mapping and GIS links.

Massachusetts

www.state.ma.us/mgis/vwr_scm.htm

MassGIS: ArcView Demonstration Movies. The site also provides data and Data Viewer and Watershed Tools specific to Massachusetts.

National Spatial Data Infrastructure

www.fgdc.gov

National Spatial Data Infrastructure (NSDI) is a centralized clearinghouse for digital geospatial data developed by a nineteen-member interagency Federal Geographic Data Committee. The NDSI encompasses policies, standards, and procedures for organizations to cooperatively produce and share geographic data, including a new section that addresses Homeland Security and GIS.

New Hampshire

docs.unh.edu/nhtopos/nhtopos.htm

University of New Hampshire, Dimond Library has historic USGS topographic maps of New England available as images.

www.granit.sr.unh.edu
New Hampshire GRANIT provides access to statewide GIS data. You can either search through their metadata database, browse the data catalog to find the layers you need, or use the Create a Map feature to make your own map.

Spatial Climate Analysis Service
www.climatesource.com
High quality, up-to-date spatial climate data sets developed by the PRISM climate mapping system at Oregon State University's Spatial Climate Analysis Service (SCAS). Climate elements include: mean monthly, and annual precipitation; temperature and humidity; freeze dates, growing, heating, and cooling degree days; precipitation and temperature extremes; and snowfall statistics. Data sets are available for all fifty U.S. states and Puerto Rico, Western Canada, Mainland China, Taiwan, and Mongolia.

Texas
www.tnris.org
Texas Natural Resources Information System (TNRIS): The state's clearinghouse for natural resources data, including water resources, geology, census, and other natural resources spatial data.

United States Geological Survey
water.usgs.gov/realtime.html
USGS Real-Time Water Data is an interactive map of real-time hydrologic data. Data for a particular station can be viewed in graph or table format. You can also download the GIS data for the real-time streamflow stations.

Vermont
crs.uvm.edu/databank.htm
Vermont Community Databank provides links to numerous sites with Vermont data (social and economic indicators, health data, census data, and population projections).

crs.uvm.edu/schlrpt/index.htm
Vermont School Reports: The data contained in the VT School Report is available for download.
www.vcgi.org
The Vermont Geographic Information System allows a user to download publicly available Vermont GIS data (boundaries, land use, 911, pollution, and lots more).

Visible Earth
Visibleearth.nasa.gov
NASA's Visible Earth: Access over 1,400 satellite images of the earth. Categories exist for agriculture, atmosphere, biosphere, cryosphere, human dimensions, hydro-sphere, land surface, oceans, radiance of imagery, solid earth, and satellites/sensors.

Web resources: Global positioning systems (GPS)

Aerospace Corporation
www.aero.org/publications/GPSPRIMER
The Aerospace Corporation's Web page provides a primer on useful GPS background information in both PDF and HTML format.

Colorado
www.colorado.Edu/geography/gcraft/notes/gps/gps_f.html
The Geographer's Craft, from the University of Colorado at Boulder, provides extensive information for a complete overview of GPS.

Garmin Corporation
www.garmin.com
The Garmin Web site provides general GPS information in addition to Garmin product information and technical support.

Magellan
www.magellangps.com/en/about
Magellan GPS product information and support.

Smithsonian
www.nasm.edu/galleries/gps/si.html
GPS at the Smithsonian gives background GPS information with several in-depth discussions ranging from "Before GPS" to "New Frontiers in Science."

TopoZone
www.topozone.com
Use TopoZone to determine the latitude and longitude coordinates of your location in decimal degrees.

Trimble
www.trimble.com
Trimble product information, technical support, and tutorials on GPS background information.

United States Navy
sirius.chinalake.navy.mil/satpred
Navy's Interactive GPS Satellite Prediction: Input your latitude, longitude, altitude, and time of day when you will be taking GPS readings in order to predict the availability of satellites and the predicted error. Use it to schedule GPS data collection for the more optimal times, in particular when the site is under heavy forest cover.

Web resources: Online maps and mapping tools

American Memory Historical Collections
memory.loc.gov/ammem/ammemhome.html
American Memory Historical Collections for the National Digital Library. Be sure to check out the Geography and Map Division, with collections of historic maps viewable as images.

Cartographic Creation of New England
www.usm.maine.edu/%7Emaps/exhibit2
The Cartographic Creation of New England. View wonderful historic maps at this University of Southern Maine Web site displaying an exhibition of early maps. The exhibit chronicles the effects of European exploration and settlement in northeastern North America.

Census Bureau Factfinder
factfinder.census.gov/servlet/BasicFactsServlet
U.S. Census Bureau FactFinder generates maps or tables from a variety of census data (population, housing, race). Users can select a particular state, county, or city to map.

Community Mapping Assistance Project
www.cmap.nypirg.org
The Community Mapping Assistance Project (CMAP) provides customized computer mapping services to nonprofit organizations across New York and nationwide. CMAP is a project of the New York Public Interest Research Group Fund, Inc. (NYPIRG).

Earth and Moon Viewer
www.fourmilab.to/earthview
Earth and Moon viewer is capable of generating custom maps using variable parameters.

Environmental Defense Fund Scorecard
www.scorecard.org
This Environmental Defense Fund Scorecard site allows you to enter your ZIP Code and get a list of pollutants currently being released into your community, how much, as well as which entities are responsible.

Environmental Protection Agency
www.epa.gov/ceisweb1/ceishome/atlas/nationalatlas/nationalmaps.html
Environmental Protection Agency (EPA) Map Links provide access to numerous environmental maps, organized by air, land, and water.

www.epa.gov/airnow
EPA's AIRNOW provides maps and animations showing air quality—particularly ozone levels.
www.epa.gov/enviro/html/em/index.html
EPA's EnviroMapper lets kids create their own maps, down to the square mile, of anywhere in America, choosing various features from water discharges to hazardous waste to roads. The site includes reports and maps of EPA's activities in your area.

ESRI
www.esri.com/mapmuseum
Map Book Gallery: Highlights of GIS maps created in numerous disciplines by users from around the world.
www.esri.com/hazards
FEMA and ESRI have formed a partnership in part aimed at providing multihazard maps and information to U.S. residents, business owners, schools, community groups, and local governments via the Internet. Use the Online Hazard Maps feature to generate maps displaying natural hazards such as floods, wind storms, and earthquakes.

Maptech
mapserver.maptech.com
The Maptech MapServer: Printable topographic, nautical, and aeronautical maps and orthophotos.

National Geographic
www.nationalgeographic.com/maps/index.html
Maps and geography.
plasma.nationalgeographic.com/mapmachine/index.html
National Geographic Map Machine generates a variety of maps and images including world physical or cultural maps, U.S. street maps, historical maps, and maps of the surface of Mars.
www.nationalgeographic.com/wildworld
National Geographic Wild World displays maps of the world's ecological regions (you can zoom in and find out about the region where you live). Also, there is a map on the world's priority areas for conservation.

National Aeronautics and Space Administration

nix.nasa.gov

NASA Image eXchange (NIX): Access over 300,000 of NASA's online image and photo collections. NIX returns thumbnail-sized images, textual descriptions, image numbers, links to higher resolution images, links to more information, and links to the NASA Center that stores each image. Images vary greatly in quality and detail, some are just handheld pictures taken out of a shuttle portal. Nonetheless, this is a good place to find imagery on a specific location or topic.

National Atlas

www.nationalatlas.gov

National Atlas delivers easy-to-use, map-like views of butterfly distributions, West Nile Virus occurrence, earthquake sites, forest fragmentation, and much more. Outstanding site with quick loading.

North American Indian Mapping

americanindian.net/links7.html

North American Indian Map Pages. This site, created by Phil Konstantin, contains many links to current and historical maps.

www.nativemaps.org
The Aboriginal Mapping Network site focuses on British Columbia, but is a resource for all First Nation mappers. Contains a map gallery and information on the native people inhabiting the Arctic National Wildlife Refuge.

Online Map Creation
www.aquarius.geomar.de/omc/make_map.html
Online Map Creation allows you to select coordinates and create your own map with features such as political boundaries, rivers, cities, and faults. The results can be saved as a postscript file.

Presidential Election Maps
fisher.lib.virginia.edu/elections/maps
United States Presidential Election Maps, 1860–1996 includes a link to 2000 presidential election information and maps.

United States Geological Survey
mac.usgs.gov/mac/isb/pubs/booklets/symbols
Topographic Map Symbols: Provides information on topographic maps and reading topographic map symbols.
water.usgs.gov/public/education.html
USGS Water Resources Education Resources is a collection of fun classroom activities that teach students about various aspects of water. There is an interactive center where students can give opinions and test their water knowledge, "FrogWeb" which focuses on amphibian declines and deformities, free education posters on wetlands and water use, and more.

Vermont
maps.vcgi.org/club
Vermont Children's Well-being features online mapping of key well-being indicators by Vermont county, school supervisory union, or school.

Off-line references

Davis, David E. 1999. *GIS for Everyone: Exploring Your Neighborhood and Your World with a Geographic Information System.* Redlands, Calif.: ESRI Press. Contains a CD with ArcExplorer™ software and 500 MB of geographic data. Access code allows users to retrieve free data from a special Web site.

Haas, Toni and Paul Nachtigal. 1998. *Place Value: An Educator's Guide to Good Literature on Rural Lifeways, Environments, and Purposes of Education.* Huntington, WV: Chapman Printing Co. Publication of ERIC Clearinghouse on Rural Education and Small Schools, operated by the Appalachia Educational Laboratory, POB 1348, Charleston, WV 25325.

Orr, David W. 1994. *Earth in Mind: On Education, Environment, and the Human Prospect.* Washington, D.C.: Island Press.

Sobel, David E. 1998. *Mapmaking with Children: Sense of Place Education for the Elementary Years.* Portsmouth, N.H.: Heinemann—a Division of Reed Elsevier, Inc.

Appendix

1 Low-end budget with cost reduction caption

2 High-end budget

3 Educator needs form

4 Project description form

Community Mapping Project Start-up Budget

For a Two-Person Educator Team

Category	Item	Description	Low Est	High Est
Educator training	**Tuition — CM Institute**	Two educators for 5-6 days	$1,000	$2,000
*Send 2 educators to CM Training Center**	**Travel expenses**	Air fare, ground travel, lodging, meals for two, miscellaneous	$2,200	$3,000
OR: 1 educator + 1 technology coordinator	**Graduate credits**	Optional – school or educator may cover costs (approx. 3 credits x 2)	$0	$400
☐		**SUBTOTAL**	**$3,200**	**$5,400**
Project Support	**GIS software**	Optional – $500/school site license (or free through Orton/ESRI incentive program)	$0	$500
	Teacher substitutes	Optional – cover for field trips, review meetings, public presentations	$0	$2,000
	GIS consultant(s)	Technical support – project design and GIS preparations, classroom assistance, data collection assistance (school technology coordinator, if trained in GIS, may be able to provide this support)	$0	$2,500
	School transportation	Optional – to/from field sites, review meetings, related events	$0	$500
		SUBTOTAL	**$0**	**$5,500**
	TOTAL	Two-educator team is trained and carries out a Community Mapping Project	**$3,200**	**$10,900**

Estimates reflect the 2003 economy and very generalized rates that may vary or change.

*Community Mapping Training Centers are currently located in Colorado and Vermont.

Ways to reduce or minimize project and training costs:

1. Seek educational scholarships and grants to cover workshop-related costs
2. Drive to training center vs. fly (if feasible)
3. Stay in dormitory facilities if available
4. Rent a condo and prepare own meals (generally more cost-effective for larger groups)
5. Send the school technology coordinator to training for purposes of providing GIS support to educators and students (vs. hiring an outside expert)
6. Take advantage of the Orton/ESRI ArcView school site license program (i.e., complete CM training and a CM project with your students)
7. Have other teachers assist with trips, classes, and events to avoid having to hire substitute teachers
8. Involve parents and school administrators in project activities — ask them to help supervise and transport students to and from project sites
9. Other _____

Community Mapping Program — Chart of potential start-up budget items

Category	Item	Description	Low Est	High Est
Program management	**Program manager**	Salary and benefits, contract fees (PT or FT)		
	Project coordinator	Salary and benefits, contract fees (PT or FT)		
	Operations (local)	Mileage, supplies, telephone, postage, rent, utilities		
	Printing and publicity	Brochure development and reproduction and ads		
	Travel (conferences, meetings)	Lodging, transportation, meals, conference fees		
	GIS expert	Salary/Fees — program development, presentations, meetings		
	Fundraiser	Grant writer and other fundraising events and contacts		
	Administrative assistant	Optional assistance		
	Graduate student intern	Optional assistance (PT)		
	Graduate credit admin	Administers teacher graduate credits and recertification		
	Curriculum consultant(s)	Program model; project integration into curricula		
	Review meeting	Optional — room rental, refreshments, subs, mileage		
	Software	GIS, extensions, Web page builder, other		
	Hardware (buy vs rent)	Laptop, PCs, LCD projector, map plotter		
		SUBTOTAL		
Training Option #1 *Assumes new CMP holds local workshops*	**GIS instructor(s)**	Fees – two five-day GIS summer workshops		
	Curriculum consultant(s)	Fees – project mgt and assessment training (three days)		
	Operations	Lab rent, perks, printing/copying, publicity		
	Training supplies	Notebooks, texts, data CDs, GPS units, batteries		
	Teacher scholarships	Optional incentive — reduced tuition		
	Teacher stipends	Optional incentive — no tuition and $100/day/person		
	Refreshments/Snacks	Optional incentive — splurging recommended		
	REVENUE—TUITION	$500/pers GIS; $125/pers project mgt and assessment		
		SUBTOTAL		
Training Option #2 *Send trainers to remote workshops*	**Tuition — GIS training**	2–6 persons for 5 days		
	Tuition — project mgt	2–6 persons for 3 days		
	Travel expenses	One–two trips for 1–6 persons		
		(i.e. Off-site in Colorado or Vermont)		
		SUBTOTAL		
Project support	**Computer hardware**	Optional — grants recommended for school PCs		
	GIS software	Optional — $500/school site license		
	Teacher substitutes	Optional — cover for field trips, review meetings		
	GIS consultant(s)	Tech project preparations, guidance, training (PT)		
	School transportation	Optional — to/from field sites, review meetings		
		SUBTOTAL		
Miscellaneous future	**Internship program**	School-to-career opportunities, stipends, support		
	Project team travel	Send teachers and students to conferences		
	Web site	Web site cost; development and maintenance contract		
	Aggressive PR campaign	Program and/or training brochures and advertising		
		SUBTOTAL		
	TOTAL 1	Training Option #1		
	TOTAL 2	Training Option #2		

Estimates reflect the 1999–2001 economy and very generalized rates that may differ in other regions.

Community Mapping Program

A Program of The Orton Family Foundation

Summer - 20____ | **Educator Needs Form** | School Year 20___ - 20___

For Use In Exploring A Community-School Partnership

Scope Guidelines: SMALL SCALE, SIMPLE, MEETS CONTENT STANDARDS, APPROPRIATE FOR STUDENTS, FLEXIBLE DEADLINE, SPECIFIC DELIVERABLES, MEETS COMMUNITY NEEDS

School: _____ Date: _____

Primary Contact: _____ Discipline: _____

Mailing Address: _____

E-mail Address: _____ Tel: _____

Other Teachers on Team   Grade(s)   Discipline(s)

_____   _____   _____

_____   _____   _____

_____   _____   _____

_____   _____   _____

Which content standards would or could be involved in a community-school mapping project?

[ ] Reading & Writing   [ ] History   [ ] Geography   [ ] Civics   [ ] Music
[ ] Mathematics (specify areas): _____
[ ] Science (specify areas): _____
[ ] Economics   [ ] Foreign Language   [ ] Physical Education   [ ] Visual Arts
[ ] Other _____   [ ] Other _____

Which SCANS competencies would or could be involved in a community-school mapping project?

[ ] Resources   [ ] Interpersonal   [ ] Information   [ ] Systems   [ ] Technology
        [ ] Basic Skills   [ ] Thinking Skills   [ ] Personal Qualities

Which units or lesson plans might easily involve spatial relationships or mapping components next year? When will these be taught?

With which community organizations are you interested in exploring project possibilities?

List specific projects you know about and are interested in exploring:

What do you think about having community mentors work with students (i.e.; pros and cons)? What experience have you had working with mentors?

How would/could you use GIS &/or GPS with students as tools to enhance their exploration and understanding of spatial topics?

How would/could you use manual mapping (i.e.; plotting points, contouring, making graphs and charts, etc.) with students as a tool to enhance their exploration and understanding of spatial topics?

How many students and teachers might be involved in carrying out a project?

How much class time could be devoted to a school-community project next year?

Will you be able to transport students to field sites or community facilities? (Explain logistics).

List the computer hardware and software resources plus other equipment that would be available for project use, (i.e.; GPS units, digital cameras, plotter, media equipment, etc.).

Who else in your school will be available during the school year to:

1) Provide technical support &/or training?
2) Lead skills development training & activities?
3) Ensure that community commitments & deadlines are met?
4) Ensure that ongoing communication occurs among all project team members?

Is your team willing to meet with the community partner to plan the project in advance of its implementation?

How about participating in a Community Mapping workshop to learn GIS basics and gain insights on how to effectively integrate the project into your curriculum?

*H*opes: *F*ears:

Community **M**apping **P**rogram

A Program of The Orton Family Foundation

Summer - 20____   **Project Description Form**   School Year
                                                                                        20____ - 20____

For Use In Exploring A Community-School Partnership

*Scope Guidelines: SMALL SCALE, SIMPLE, RELATES TO SCHOOL SUBJECT(S), APPROPRIATE FOR
STUDENTS, FLEXIBLE DEADLINE, SPECIFIC DELIVERABLES, MEETS COMMUNITY NEEDS*

Community Organization: _____ Date: _____

Contact Name: _____ Tel: _____

Mailing Address: _____

E-mail Address: _____

Briefly describe the project your organization would like developed that involves spatial
relationships or mapping.

What *question(s)* or *issue(s)* does this project address?

What specific, tangible products could students help you develop?

How will the products or project results be used?

DATA
[ ] **Existing data is available**   ⇨   **What data?** _____

   Where is it? _____ **Resolution:** _____

[ ] **Data collection required**   ⇨   **What data?** _____

   How much? _____ **Resolution:** _____

Special data needs/concerns:

By *when* do you need different phases of the project completed?

Where is the project setting located?

Which disciplines would be involved?

[ ] Social/Cultural   [ ] Economics   [ ] Environmental   [ ] History
[ ] Mathematics   [ ] Life Sciences   [ ] Physical Sciences   [ ] Civics
[ ] Music   [ ] Geography   [ ] Physical Education   [ ] Reading & Writing
[ ] Visual Arts   [ ] Communications   [ ] Foreign Language   [ ] Technology
[ ] Other _____   [ ] Other _____
[ ] Other _____   [ ] Other _____

What are the benefits to your organization from involving students in your work?

***Who* will be available during the school year to:**
1) **Provide overall guidance & direction?**
2) **Work with students & teachers to identify & meet curriculum objectives through your issue/project?**
3) **Develop *mentoring* relationships with students in the classroom & the field?**

What other community resources (e.g.; people & equipment) would need to be recruited?

*H*opes:

*F*ears:

Please fill out and return to: _____

_____